Feeling Your Feelings from the Bottom Up

A Somatic Guide to Understanding and Integrating Core Emotions Through the Body

Tiffany Todd, LCSW

ISBN 979-8-234-05038-0

Cover design by Hannah Fitch

Fannie Pearl Press

Chicago, Illinois

Printed on acid free paper in the

United States of America

This book is dedicated to my Mama. This is the book I wish I could have given her.

A Word About Safety

I think it is important to note before starting this book or trying the exercises, trauma can hijack the nervous system. I am personally in therapy and believe everyone should have a therapist; it is never shameful to ask for help. I also know not everyone has the privilege of therapeutic access so these resources should serve as a starting point for deeper work.

Throughout this text, we will be discussing themes of safety. The focus here is on emotional safety.

Emotional safety is the felt experience of being able to notice, express, and allow your emotions without fear of judgment, punishment, or abandonment, from others or from yourself. Emotional safety does not ask you to strive for a state of perfection or emotional neutrality. It is the internal sense that whatever arises within you can be met with curiosity, compassion, and steadiness. Emotional safety allows you to stay present with the full range of your emotional experience without needing to reject, minimize, or over-control it. In the context of healing, emotional safety becomes the foundation for building tolerance to discomfort, exploring beliefs, and shifting patterns that once served as survival strategies. It starts in the body, where the nervous system signals that you are safe enough to feel, and expands into the relationship you form with yourself as you gently re-learn that emotions are messengers, not threats.

In cases of genuine danger, such as being in an abusive relationship, not having basic needs met, or facing threats to your well-being, attempting to change your perception of safety is not only ineffective, it can be harmful. It is neither safe nor helpful to affirm safety when you are genuinely at risk.

The nervous system operates on scale between the extreme states of hyperarousal (fight/flight) and hypoarousal (shutdown). In between these extremes is an optimal zone of emotional arousal in which a person can think clearly, regulate emotions, and respond effectively. This optimal zone is known as the window of tolerance. Nervous system dysregulation is defined as impaired autonomic flexibility where the nervous system remains stuck in hyperarousal or hypoarousal, outside the window of tolerance, instead of fluidly responding to safety and threat. It can sometimes mimic health conditions and health conditions can sometimes mimic dysregulation. A medical check-in is a good companion to emotional work.

Introduction

Stop.

Before reading further, pause for just a moment.

Notice your body. The place where you are supported. The contact of your feet with the floor, your back against the chair, your hands resting where they are. You may notice tension, ease, restlessness, or very little at all. There is no right way to experience this.

We begin here, with what your body is already doing.

"People may not have caused all of our own problems, but they have to solve them anyway." – Marsha Linehan

I am sorry to be the bearer of bad news, but you are a human, experiencing human life with all the emotions that entails. You are made to laugh and cry and scream and startle and recoil and run if you need to protect yourself. You are meant to rage against injustice and mourn your losses.

You will experience anger, fear, sadness, disgust, surprise, and enjoyment in all their glorious variations. Sometimes these feelings may overwhelm, feel distant, or you might feel stuck in the feelings. But there is good news! Much of our distress comes from our attempts to not be so terribly human. We don't want to feel our feelings. We want to control, avoid, reject, fight, and get rid of them.

I get it. These intense feelings can be quite unpleasant. The tightness in the chest. The tingly skin. The pit in the stomach.

You may be aware of your struggle with your emotions or think you handle them just fine. You may be actively working to shift your responses toward your preferred responses. Or you may feel aware and trapped in the same patterns.

If you have ever understood something logically but still felt stuck emotionally, you are not alone.

Perhaps you sit in your car before walking into work, knowing the meeting is safe, telling yourself you are prepared, capable, fine. And still your heart races, your palms sweat, your jaw tightens. You rehearse what you will say in case something goes wrong.

Or maybe it happens in the middle of a conversation. Your partner says something neutral. A shift in tone. A pause. Suddenly your stomach drops. Heat rises in your face. Shame or anger floods in before you understand why. You know you are loved. Your body reacts as if you are not.

The mind says one thing. The body says another.

For now, I would ask you to suspend your thinking of things. This may not be the easiest thing to do. Thinking may be your go-to strategy. It could even be a true strength. I get it, I'm a thinker too. But insight alone rarely shifts a nervous system state.

We will instead view our body and mind through the lens of the six core emotions: enjoyment, sadness, anger, fear, disgust, and surprise. We all experience these emotions and it gives us a clear entry point into what the nervous system is doing and how it shapes our experience.

This work asks you to explore from the bottom up, starting with increasing awareness of what your body is doing. You will learn to notice nervous system states, identify emotions, and connect them to your felt experience. You will practice regulating the experience of emotion in the present moment and tending to it regardless of the cause or how sensible or not it may seem.

And then, and only then, we will explore and address the thoughts and beliefs that grow out of these states and reinforce them.

This is not a book to rush through. Much of this work happens slowly, in small moments of noticing. It often benefits from returning to the same practices more than once.

Ideally, we want to experience the emotions of life, both pleasant and unpleasant, without a shift in how we view the worth of self or our overall view of others and the world.

With a shift in how we view symptoms as protective instead of problems, how we respond mentally and physically to them, and a deeper understanding of why the tools work, I believe there is a steadier path to healing. One that builds internal trust and begins where you actually live, in your body

The ability to be in the present moment is a major component of mental wellness. – Abraham Maslow

To live in the present moment is a miracle. The miracle is not to walk on water. The miracle is to walk on the green earth in the present moment, to appreciate the peace and beauty that are available now. – Thich Nhat Hanh

"When you are born," the golem said softly, "your courage is new and clean. You are brave enough for anything: crawling off of staircases, saying your first words without fearing that someone will think you are foolish, putting strange things in your mouth. But as you get older, your courage attracts gunk, and crusty things, and dirt, and fear, and knowing how bad things can get and what pain feels like. By the time you're half-grown, your courage barely moves at all, it's so grunged up with living. So every once in awhile, you have to scrub it up and get the works going, or else you'll never be brave again." – Catherynne M. Valente, The Girl Who Circumnavigated Fairyland in a Ship of Her Own Making

Bring awareness to your experience

Objective: Understand and bring awareness to body states.

Awareness

Knowledge or perception of a situation or fact.

Let's pretend for a moment that you are a newly formed human, a newborn, if you will. Can you imagine yourself there in the distance? Naked, shiny, without the thick weight of the world layered upon you? Maybe you are screaming, having just been pushed out into chaos, deprived of the soothing rhythms of your mother's body. You are certainly feeling your feelings. Of course, you are.

Nothing is known to you in this newly created moment in your newly created body. You have no knowledge or associations. You are exposed to a flood of sensations, but have not labeled or tied meaning to them. Instead, a newborn lives perfectly in the moment, strong feelings and all.

The world is infinite before you and filled with all possibilities. We will start there with curiosity.

Curiosity

A strong desire to learn or know something. An aroused interest.

Radical acceptance rests on letting go of the illusion of control and a willingness to notice and accept things as they are right now, without judging. – Marsha Linehan

Radical Acceptance is the willingness to experience ourselves and our lives as it is. – Tara Branch

What Is My Body Doing?

Present moment awareness

The conscious, open attention to what is happening right now, both internally and externally, without judgment or distraction. It's the act of sensing, feeling, and noticing experience as it unfolds, just as it is, rather than getting pulled into the past or future by meaning-making.

When we enter the world, we exist fully in the present moment. We have no mental framework for the world we find ourselves in. There is no story yet about who we are or how things work. There is sensation, light, sound, warmth, hunger, and contact. We respond as we perceive.

As we begin interacting with our environment, impressions start to form. Sensations are registered through our five senses: sight, sound, touch, taste, and smell. Experiences accumulate, and meaning slowly attaches itself to what we perceive. These sensory experiences do not happen in isolation but in relationship. A cry is heard and answered, or it is not. A need is soothed through touch and tone, or it lingers in the body. A smile is reflected back through eye contact and expression, or it falls into empty space. Through thousands of repeated sensory exchanges, patterns organize. The nervous system learns what to expect from the world and from others. Over time, beliefs take shape.

There is a reason the brain works this way.

Each second, the nervous system takes in far more information than we can consciously process. To function efficiently, the brain filters and condenses input, relying on past experience to predict what will happen next. Without this predictive ability, every moment would require new interpretation, and we would quickly become overwhelmed.

After sensory input is detected and before the thinking mind has time to interpret, the body responds. Information first moves through lower brain structures, including the amygdala, which can initiate shifts before signals reach the prefrontal cortex. We may notice tightness in the chest, a drop in the stomach, muscle tension, or a change in breath or heart rate before we consciously understand why. The state shifts first, and the explanation follows.

But prediction comes with a consequence. Over time, repeated emotional experiences solidify into embodied expectation. If comfort reliably follows distress, the body learns that activation can settle. If anger is met with punishment or withdrawal, the body may learn that anger is dangerous. If sadness is ignored, the body may learn to suppress it. As these patterns repeat, they organize into a framework that is not simply ideas about the world, but lived, physiological anticipation. Even when the rational mind understands the present context, the body may still register threat, rejection, or vulnerability. Thinking alone does not override a nervous system that has already mobilized. The body feels first, and it feels deeply.

These embodied frameworks are what we later come to call beliefs. They are not simply thoughts we carry, but conclusions reinforced through repeated emotional and physiological experience. Over time, they shape how we interpret sensation, assign meaning, and anticipate what will happen next. Some support flexibility and connection. Others were formed in moments of overwhelm, misattunement, or pain and now quietly narrow what feels safe to experience.

Because beliefs are sustained through bodily repetition, they rarely shift through insight alone. The body participates in maintaining them. A bottom-up approach works by changing lived physiological experience. When the body begins to experience safety, steadiness, and completion, beliefs soften. New perspectives emerge not because we forced new thoughts, but because the internal state has changed.

This is why we begin with awareness. Before we analyze the story, we pause and ask: *What is my body doing?*

As awareness grows, you will begin connecting these responses to the core emotions of fear, sadness, anger, disgust, surprise, and enjoyment.

Viktor Frankl wrote, "Between stimulus and response, there is a space. In that space lies our freedom and power to choose." Awareness creates the space. The nervous system moves quickly, so that space can feel nearly invisible.

We do not find it by thinking harder. We meet the body first, with curiosity instead of judgment. As we learn to notice and turn toward our internal state, the space widens. In that widening, new choices become embodied, not just understood.

Life is happening now, in the child laughing outside your window, the bee hovering over a blooming flower, the clouds drifting overhead. Come back to the present moment that's still here, waiting for you.

Nervous System 101

The body constantly moves through different states of the autonomic nervous system, responding to our felt sense of safety or threat. These states, ventral vagal, sympathetic, and dorsal vagal, are organized in a hierarchy shaped by our evolutionary need to survive. This is the heart of Dr. Stephen Porges' polyvagal theory.

The ventral vagal state, sometimes called the social engagement system, is where we feel anchored and open. In this state, the ventral vagal complex is active, softening the body into ease. Heartbeat steady, muscles relaxed but awake, breath flowing in a smooth rhythm, digestion working as it should. Here, we feel able to reach outward, to connect, to play, to listen and speak freely.

When something feels threatening, the body shifts into sympathetic activation, mobilizing us for action. Energy surges while the heart rate climbs; the breath quickens and muscles tighten. It's a readiness response for either fight or flight. Emotionally, this can feel like urgency, frustration, anxiety, or even restlessness. The body is asking: *What must I do to survive?*

But if the threat feels like too much to bear, the system may drop into the dorsal vagal state, a deep withdrawal. Here, the body slows to protect itself. The heart rate drops, breath becomes shallow, muscles feel heavy or limp. It can feel like moving through fog, disconnected and numb. Our energy fades, and we may feel invisible, collapsed, or frozen, still within the parasympathetic system, but at the lowest ebb of its cycle.

The Window Of Tolerance

The window of tolerance is our internal range of felt safety. Within it, we move fluidly through emotions and sensations, meeting life with steadiness and curiosity. Dr. Dan Siegel first named this concept in 1999, describing the zone where we function best, thinking clearly, feeling deeply, and responding with care.

Inside our window, our breath feels smooth and steady, deepening when needed. Muscles hold us comfortably, not too tight, not too loose. Our stomach feels settled. The jaw softens; our face opens. We're grounded, aware of the floor beneath our feet, the air around us. Our energy balances between rest and alertness, keeping us engaged but not overwhelmed.

In this place, the prefrontal cortex is available, helping us plan, organize, focus, and regulate emotions. We can reflect on what is important to us, align with our values, and make choices that consider both ourselves and others.

But our window of tolerance is not fixed. It flexes and shifts depending on life experience, present circumstances, and what we've learned about emotions, especially in childhood. Early emotional learnings, formed during moments of intense feeling, shape how wide or narrow our window becomes. These learnings are often implicit, absorbed without conscious effort, woven into our responses over time.

Because the window is subjective, it belongs to you. You get to notice what feels right, what feels like too much, and what feels like too little. Trauma and the beliefs born from it can narrow this window, making certain emotions feel unbearable or hard to stay with. Just notice what comes up. You are simply observing. Nothing has gone wrong. You are safe in the present moment. Everyone moves in and out of their window at times. What is important is noticing with kindness.

Outside The Window Of Tolerance

Hyperarousal

When the body senses danger, it may be pushed into hyperarousal, led by the sympathetic nervous system. Heart racing, breath quick and shallow, muscles tight and ready. Digestion slows as energy is rerouted for survival. Thoughts may race, loop, or skew negative, making focus difficult. The mind feels pulled into urgency, the body primed for action or defense. In hyperarousal, we move beyond the window of tolerance, carried by the storm of activation.

Hypoarousal

When a threat feels overwhelming or escape feels impossible, the body may drop into hypoarousal, the dorsal vagal response of shutdown. Heart rate slows, breath becomes faint or shallow, muscles lose tone. Your thought processes may feel clouded, as if moving through heavy mist. There can be a sense of detachment from self and surroundings, a fading from view. In this state, we're well outside the window of tolerance, conserving energy, trying to disappear from threat.

Our nervous system flows between these states, responding moment by moment to the perceived landscape of safety and danger. As threats ease, the body can rise from immobility into sympathetic energy, then settle back into the calm rhythm of the ventral vagal state. This is the path back to balance, back to ourselves.

For our purposes, we will refer to these states as window of tolerance, hyperarousal, and hypoarousal throughout the rest of the text.

Mapping Your Window Of Tolerance

This exercise will help you create a personal representation of your window, a space where you feel regulated and able to engage with life.

Define Your Window

Find a quiet space. Take a few slow breaths and bring to mind times when you've felt balanced, clear-headed, and in control of your emotions. Picture a time when you felt at ease, connected with your core self, and fully present in the moment. Maybe you felt safe, alert, calm, and capable. *How did this feel in your body? Were your limbs relaxed, slightly heavy, loose? Were your thoughts steady and focused? Did you feel connected to the present moment?*

Remember, being in your window doesn't mean only experiencing preferred emotions. It means having the capacity to feel and process any emotion, sadness, anger, joy, fear, without becoming overwhelmed or shutting down.

If it's hard to recall this state, imagine someone you know or a character from a movie who embodies it. *How do they move? What is their tone of voice? How do they respond to emotions?* This sense of balance and engagement represents your window of tolerance.

Now, recall times when you've felt overwhelmed, anxious, or reactive (hyperarousal) and times when you've felt numb, disconnected, or shut down (hypoarousal). Notice gently what your body and mind are doing during these times. These states occur outside your window.

Choose a Representation

Create a visual, symbolic, or written representation of your window of tolerance. Choose one of the following methods or create your own:

Drawing or diagram: Sketch a window, river, or other shape that represents your regulation zone. Use colors, symbols, or textures to illustrate what it feels like inside vs. outside your window.

Metaphor: Describe your window as a place (a sturdy bridge, a calm ocean, a tree swaying but not breaking). How does it shift in storms or stress?

Written reflection: Write a brief description of what it's like to be inside your window, what pushes you out, and what helps you return.

Identify Cues and Supports

In your representation, include:

Signs you're in your window: Steady breathing, clear thinking, emotional flexibility.

Signs you're outside your window: Racing thoughts, muscle tension, shutdown.

Resources that help you return: Movement, grounding techniques, co-regulation, sensory engagement.

Reflect and Adjust

Your window of tolerance is not fixed, it can expand with awareness and practice. Revisit your representation over time, noticing what helps you stay within it and what shifts your experience.

Observing Your Experience

Objective: Begin noticing internal shifts

A word on resistance: Emotional resistance is an internal block that prevents full engagement with emotions. It arises when the mind resists acknowledging feelings, often due to past experiences or discomfort with vulnerability. Notice resistance when it appears; it provides valuable information about your body's responses. Take the smallest step toward it. Any amount of noticing, in whatever way feels safe to notice, is a step towards.

You are the observer. An observer watches and notices.

The following exercises help reconnect with the physical self, increasing awareness of the body's state and its responses to stimuli. You do not have to complete every exercise, or any at all, to achieve this goal. If something feels overwhelming, trust yourself and skip it. Learning to trust your body's cues is part of the process. If none of these resonate, explore your own ways of connecting with your felt experience.

It's normal if noticing feels unfamiliar, strange, or even uncomfortable at first. Especially if you've spent a long time tuned outward or managing strong emotions, turning inward can feel tender. Start wherever you are, without judgment.

These exercises invite you to rest in this exact moment, setting aside meaning-making, past, future, and analysis, for now.

Practice

(noun) Application or use of an idea, belief or method, as opposed to theories related to it.

(verb) Perform an activity or exercise a skill repeatedly and/or regularly in order to improve or maintain one's proficiency.

A note on practice: All forms of learning require practice and repetition to increase skill. Walking, talking, reading, writing, regulating our bodies, and even feeling our feelings all require practice. As you begin using these exercises and concepts, it is normal for the body to need practice.

Simple Present Moment Awareness (Senses)

Pause for a moment here and notice all the sensory input your nervous system is taking in right now. Your feet may be touching the floor. Were you noticing that before? What else is your body touching? The back of your thighs against the chair? The fabric of your clothing against your skin? The temperature of the air on your arms? What sensations were already present but outside of your awareness until now?

Move gently into what you can see. What is directly in your line of vision? What colors, shapes, or textures stand out? Now, shift your awareness to your peripheral vision, objects, shadows, or light that you weren't consciously registering before. How does the space around you reveal itself as you take it in with fresh attention?

Can you hear anything? The hum of an appliance, the murmur of voices in another room, the rhythmic pattern of your own breath. Maybe silence has a texture of its own, a quiet weight in the space around you.

What about scent? The faint trace of soap on your skin, the earthy smell of rain drifting in through an open window, the lingering aroma of coffee or tea. Some smells might go unnoticed until they become the center of awareness. Others may pull you into memory, stirring emotions or recalling forgotten moments.

And finally, taste. Even if you haven't eaten recently, is there a subtle taste in your mouth? The remnants of toothpaste, the sweetness of something you sipped earlier, or the neutral sensation of nothing at all?

Sensations are rarely just physical. Often, they are the first language of your emotional self, telling you through heat, tightness, fluttering, or stillness that something inside is shifting.

Each of these senses is constantly offering input, grounding you in this moment. Notice what it's like to simply be here in this moment.

How to Move Into the Body: You Are the Observer

This exercise will push your tolerance of feeling the physical sensations/emotions/feelings just a bit more. Think of it as a stretch in yoga: can I lean into it just a little bit further? Only push a tiny bit more than you are comfortable with.

Take a moment to get comfortable, whatever feels comfortable to you. Allow your body to settle into the chair or the surface where you are reclining, your breathing slow, natural. Just observe with curiosity. Notice the support your body is receiving underneath you, allowing yourself to relax into it. Let yourself sink into observer mode. You can close your eyes or leave them open and soften your gaze. Breathing into the sense of relaxation and safety in this present moment.

Continue to turn your attention inwards and embody the observer noticing what you are experiencing with curiosity and the acceptance of your newly formed self.

There may be thoughts floating by as you observe, we are going to just notice them for now and allow ourselves to release our tight grip on them with a promise to come back later. Notice them floating off with compassion. Take a moment to acknowledge yourself with love, a human in a body being human. Notice any resistance that comes up with curiosity and acceptance. Sit with it for a moment, breathing into and out of the resistance. Allow only a small bit more than is comfortable. Gently notice the fullness in your head as you embody the observer, breathing deeply in and out. Just noticing, with curiosity and acceptance.

Now bring your awareness from the space in your head, feel it become a defined point in the middle of your crown and move forward down the center of your forehead, spreading smoothness across. Moving down the slope of your nose and off the tip, across your lips and down your chin. Imagine your observer moving down your neck in whatever way feels comfortable. I like to think of mine swirling around the outside of my neck all the way down and all the way up, clearing out the emotions that get stuck there. You might imagine the beam of a flashlight moving from the space in your head down your body into your core. Maybe your observer is a soothing purple light that lights up as you notice. Moving your observer in whatever way feels comfortable and safe into your physical body. Moving away from the thoughts in the head space.

What does your observer have curiosity about as it moves into your physical body? Does your observer sense tension? What other physical sensations are there? Allow your observer to scan the body with curiosity and acceptance. Does your observer try to move back toward thought? Gently redirect back into the body with curiosity. Stay with body sensations as much as you can, allowing your observer to explore your physical body starting with your toes and moving upwards scanning as you go. Notice your lungs filling with air as your observer explores any sensations in your body. Continue to breathe at your own pace. In and out.

Notice and allow any sensations you find. Tingling, tension, warmth, cold, numbness, pulsating, or any other sensations. Continue to breathe as you scan your body, noticing without judgment. Do not move into solving. Allow what you can, just a tiny bit more than feels comfortable, not pushing away, breathing into it. Just noticing. It was already there, nothing has changed just yet. Continue to focus on your breathing, noticing the movement of your chest as you breathe. You can stay here in your body as long as you would like. When you feel comfortable and ready to re-engage, slowly open and focus your eyes and give your body a slow stretch.

Things To Observe In Your Body

Keep in mind that there are many body sensations and none are right or wrong. Notice each with curiosity using the guide below.

Questions to Ask Yourself

Is there anything drawing my attention in my body?

Am I noticing any sensations in my body?

Were any of these sensations expressing a need?

Did I answer the need or push it away?

What could I allow?

Do I have any tension in my jaw, feet, shoulders, hip, neck, or other areas?

Do I notice a sense of numbness or disconnection in my body?

Do I notice a sense of anxiety or activation in my body?

Do I equate a word or emotion to what I am feeling in my body?

Is there an image, color or visual representation you relate to the noticed sensations?

Areas to Notice

Scalp, forehead eyes, jaw, mouth, face

Neck, throat, shoulders

Arms, wrists, hands, fingers

Chest, lungs

Stomach, gut, trunk, spine

Hips, pelvic area, bottom

Thighs, knees, calves, ankles, feet and toes

Common Sensations: warmth, cold, tingling, trembling, quaking, heart-pounding, irregular heart feelings/beats, increased awareness of pulse, sweating, feeling clammy, feeling open, feeling closed off, shuttered, numb, energized, startled, clenching, tension, feeling loose, relaxed, hollow, heavy, etc.

> If you are feeling extreme resistance here, heightened feelings of anxiety and/or experiencing a sense of shut down, I encourage you to start there and consider finding a therapist to guide you through the process. If you do not have access to a therapist, begin with establishing safety in self.
>
> We all experience forms of resistance to sensations and emotions and while these sensations and emotions can inform us, these exercises are not meant to cause high levels of distress. Trust yourself and your tolerance.

Awareness of the signs of each state is a key first step in this process.

Our new human self feels a sense of attraction and withdrawal to these first sensations. We are attracted to pleasant sensations that bring comfort, pleasure, and stimulation and withdraw from unpleasant sensations such as pain or unappealing flavors. We are fully in the present moment of exactly what is happening in front of us and demanding our caregivers meet our needs and teach us what these sensations are all about and healthy ways to respond to what we are experiencing.

End-Of-Chapter Practice: Listening To The Body

This week, gently bring your awareness to the shifts in your body. Notice how your physical state fluctuates, moving up into tension, urgency, or activation, or down into stillness, heaviness, or withdrawal. Let your curiosity lead, without judgment.

When you feel a change, ask:

- Am I thinking this, or feeling it?
- If I'm thinking it, how is my body feeling it?
- What might my body need to feel more settled, more supported?

Your only job is to notice. Let yourself become more familiar with how your body responds to the world around and within you. Pay attention to the edges of your window of tolerance, that inner zone where you feel present, capable, and connected, and the subtle or sharp shifts away from it.

Notice any draw toward or retreat from your sensations. Are there moments when you avoid or resist feeling? When do you lean in? If beliefs or inner commentary arise, gently set them aside. This is not about solving or fixing. It's about noticing.

You might ask yourself:

- What does my window of tolerance feel like right now?
- If I rated it from 0 (rarely in it) to 10 (living mostly within it), what number fits today?
- How do I know when I'm in my window of tolerance? What does it feel like?
- What are my signs of hyperarousal, when my system moves into fight or flight?
- What are my signs of hypoarousal, when I shift toward shutdown or collapse?
- What would I like my window of tolerance to feel like, look like, or include?

Every bit of awareness is a return to the present moment. Every time you notice, you grow.

Bravo.

Awareness Shifting 101: Or how to notice

How Are You Experiencing Yourself And The World?

Objective: Increase ability to reconnect with the physical self, increase awareness of the body's state, response to stimuli and ability to shift between states.

Until you make the unconscious conscious, it will direct your life and you will call it fate. – Carl Jung

Awareness is like the sun. When it shines on things, they are transformed. – Thich Nhat Hanh

The following exercises are meant to help reconnect with the physical self, increasing awareness of the body's state and its responses to stimuli. You do not have to complete every exercise, or any at all, to achieve this goal. If something feels overwhelming, trust yourself and skip it. Learning to trust your body's cues is part of the process. If none of these exercises resonate, explore your own ways of connecting with your felt experience, using the concepts as a guide.

These exercises invite you to rest in this exact moment, setting aside meaning-making, the past, the future, and analysis, for now.

Where do you perceive yourself right at this moment? The part of you that is you. The part of yourself that is noticing right now. Are you in your head space? A spot on your forehead, or perhaps the top of your head. Maybe your awareness is at the back of your head. Are you a spot on your body? Does your awareness move as you think about these spots?

Is your awareness external on a worry, the past or the future? Are you in your thoughts? This might be due to reading this book or maybe you are having thoughts about something else and struggling to focus on what you are reading. Notice yourself holding both, these words and the other thoughts. As you are noticing, you are already shifting your awareness and directing it in a way you prefer.

Learning to reconnect with our ability to shift our awareness, practicing and reinforcing these skills, is a good place to begin to create a larger sense of safety in self.

Neuroception

I am capable of shifting my awareness internally and externally. I can also rest my awareness in both places at once.

I am aware that I am thinking. I am aware of the car driving by my window. And I am the observer of both.

Neuroception is a term from Dr. Stephen Porges and his polyvagal theory. This theory presents a model of the autonomic nervous system's three evolutionary states—ventral vagal (safety/social engagement), sympathetic (fight/flight), dorsal vagal (shutdown/immobility)—which are driven by neuroception of safety or threat. Neuroception describes how our nervous system, without us even realizing it, is always scanning for signs of safety or danger.

This isn't something we choose, it happens below conscious awareness. Our system is constantly reading both the world around us and the world inside us, deciding in each moment whether things feel safe, risky, or life-threatening. And from there, it adjusts our energy, lifting us into hyperarousal, pulling us down into hypoarousal, or settling us into a place where connection feels possible.

Neuroception doesn't just influence our energy levels and physical states. It also colors the emotional tone we experience. When our system senses a threat, even before we consciously realize it, emotions of fear, anger, sadness, or shutdown can rise alongside physical shifts in our body. In the same way, when safety is sensed, emotions of curiosity, playfulness, or compassion have the room to emerge.

Our nervous system relies on two main streams of information for this: exteroception and interoception.

Exteroception is what we notice from the outside world, the warmth of sunlight, the sound of someone's voice, or the sharpness of a sudden noise. These external signals tell our body about our surroundings.

Interoception is what we feel on the inside, the flutter of our heart, the ease of a deep breath, or the tension in our muscles. These internal sensations reflect how we're experiencing the moment from within.

Neuroception weaves these two together, forming an ongoing, moment-to-moment understanding of whether we are safe or need to protect ourselves. For instance, if something outside feels startling and our heart races in response, our system might swing toward hyperarousal. If the world feels too much and we begin to shut down, hypoarousal might take over. And when both outside and inside feel calm and steady, the nervous system leans into safety and connection.

Our neuroception isn't always reading the present moment clearly, however. Past experiences can shape what our body notices and how it interprets the signals. Sometimes, our system gets stuck, responding to echoes of the past instead of what's here and now.

This is why practice is essential. By noticing how we can shift between focusing on the inside or the outside, we can remind our body that it *can* shift, that it isn't trapped in one or the other. It's helpful to try this when you are within your window of tolerance, or in moments of lower activation, when it feels a bit easier to explore. Shifting your attention in these moments teaches your nervous system that flexibility is possible, building small pathways back to the present.

Please see a physician for a physical to rule out medical concerns before beginning these practices related to physical sensations.

Interoception (Internal)

I can focus my awareness on my body as a whole or specific parts of my body. I can shift my awareness from a felt sensation to my thoughts.

Interoception is the process by which we perceive internal bodily sensations. It includes the awareness of physiological states such as hunger, thirst, heartbeat, and breathing, as well as emotional states like anxiety, calmness, or excitement. Interoception helps us understand our internal condition and respond appropriately to our body's needs.

Remember our observer from chapter 1, we will bring them up now and connect with that part of us for the following exercises. We may need a reminder of our ability to direct our focus to and from things we prefer and do not prefer.

Let's explore shifting awareness together.

Inner Observer

First, turn your attention toward your thoughts. Imagine stepping back, one step away, then two, watching from a slight distance. What do your thoughts look like? Are they flowing like a river, tangled like threads, or neatly stored like files? Let an image emerge that feels right to you. There's no need to change anything, just observe.

Now, take a deep breath in ... and out. Gently shift your awareness to the big toe on your left foot. Notice the contact it makes with the ground or the air around it. Can you sense warmth, coolness, tingling, or stillness? Trace the shape of your toe with your awareness, as if outlining it in your mind.

Take another deep breath in ... and out. Now, move your awareness to the center of your chest. Feel the subtle rise and fall with each breath. Is there a sense of openness, tightness, warmth, or something else? If you don't notice anything, that's okay too, just stay present.

Now, shift your focus to your hands. Notice the sensation in your palms and fingertips. Are they warm or cool? Do they feel light, heavy, still, or slightly buzzing with energy? Perhaps you can sense the air moving across them or the surface they're resting on.

With your next breath, bring your awareness to your jaw. Is there tightness or softness? Are your teeth touching or slightly apart? Maybe there's a small movement as you breathe. Let your attention rest here briefly.

Now, let your awareness travel to the space behind your eyes. Does this area feel spacious, tense, or neutral? Simply notice.

Take another deep breath in ... and out. Slowly, bring your awareness back to your thoughts. Do they feel the same, or has something shifted? Observe without judgment, knowing you can return to this practice whenever you need.

We will give ourselves grace, patience and kindness as we practice remembering. Notice any beliefs that arise and note them for later. We will gently notice with kindness and thankfulness for the increased knowledge of ourselves and set that aside for now.

Body Scan

A full body scan can feel overwhelming if you experience strong internal sensations. It's okay to move slowly or begin with smaller practices first. If you notice discomfort or dysregulation as you begin, gently remind yourself that nothing has gone wrong. Simply noticing what arises is a form of care. Your willingness to be present with your experience, exactly as it is, is enough.

Here are some affirmations to say gently to yourself when you encounter strong felt sensations.

I can feel this sensation without fear. It is strong, but I am stronger.

This feeling is temporary, and I have the capacity to stay with it.

I make space for discomfort, knowing it will shift in its own time.

I am safe in this moment, even as my body reacts strongly.

I can notice this sensation without needing to push it away.

My body is communicating with me, and I am listening with patience.

I have endured difficult feelings before, and I can handle this one too.

I trust my body's ability to settle when it is ready.

This sensation does not define me; I am so much more than this moment.

Even in discomfort, I am here, present, and whole.

Gentle Body Scan for Increased Tolerance

These may be done all at once or only one section at a time. Whatever feels best and right for your system. Only push a tiny bit more than is comfortable. We are slowly increasing our window of tolerance and there is no rush.

Find a comfortable position, either sitting or lying down. You do not need to close your eyes unless that feels supportive. A softened gaze is enough. Take a slow breath in and allow it to leave your body naturally.

As you begin, remember that awareness does not require intensity. You can notice sensations lightly and stay at the edge of your experience rather than moving into it fully. If at any point something feels like too much, you can return to the sensation of breathing or pause the practice altogether.

Top of the Head and Forehead

Bring your attention to the top of your head and your forehead. Notice what is present here. You might sense warmth, coolness, pressure, tightness, or very little at all. There is no right sensation to find.

Let your awareness rest here for a few breaths. You are not trying to relax this area or change it. Simply notice what it is like to be aware of this part of your body. If your attention drifts, gently bring it back to the top of your head and forehead, noticing how it feels in this moment.

If this area feels activating, allow your attention to soften. You can widen your awareness slightly or return to your breath before continuing.

Face (Eyes, Jaw, Mouth)

Now bring your attention to your face. Begin with your eyes. Notice whether they feel alert, heavy, tired, or neutral. There is no need to adjust them. Just notice.

Move your awareness to your jaw and mouth. Many people hold tension here without realizing it. Notice if your jaw feels clenched, loose, or somewhere in between. Let your lips rest naturally.

Stay with this area for a few breaths, allowing sensations to exist without needing to respond to them. If it feels supportive, imagine your awareness resting gently on your face rather than focusing narrowly on any one sensation.

Neck and Shoulders

Let your attention move down to your neck and shoulders. This area often carries effort from the day. Notice what you find here. You might sense heaviness, tightness, pulling, warmth, or a sense of movement as you breathe.

You do not need to work with these sensations. Simply acknowledge them. If it feels comfortable, notice how your breath moves around this area, not into it, just nearby.

If your neck or shoulders feel intense to notice, you can keep your awareness broad, as though you are aware of the whole upper body rather than this area alone. Stay for a few steady breaths.

Hands and Fingers

Bring your attention to your hands and fingers. Notice where they are resting and how they are positioned. Feel the contact between your hands and whatever is supporting them.

Notice any sensations that stand out. This might include warmth, coolness, tingling, pulsing, or very little sensation at all. All of this is okay.

If it feels supportive, you can slowly open and close your hands once or twice, then allow them to rest again. Notice any shift that follows, even if it is subtle. Stay with your hands for a few breaths before moving on.

Feet and Toes

Finally, bring your attention to your feet and toes. Notice their weight and their contact with the floor or surface beneath you. You might sense pressure, temperature, or a feeling of steadiness.

If it feels comfortable, gently press your feet into the ground or wiggle your toes. Then pause and notice what you feel afterward. There is no need to interpret the sensation.

Allow your awareness to rest here for a few breaths. If focusing on your feet feels grounding, you can stay here longer. If not, you can gently shift your attention back to your breath.

When you are ready, allow your awareness to widen to include as much or as little of your body as feels right. You can end the practice at any point.

Create Space around Body Sensations

This exercise helps increase your capacity to create distance from strong body sensations. As sensations are allowed and experienced without resistance, the body's threat response decreases and begins to recalibrate.

Find a comfortable position, either sitting or lying down, and let your eyes close if that feels safe. Take a slow, steady breath in, then exhale, allowing your body to soften into the surface that supports you.

Bring your awareness to the part of your body where a strong sensation is present. Notice it as clearly as you can. Is it tight, heavy, restless, or sharp? Simply observe what you find without judgment.

Now imagine this sensation appearing as a color. Allow the first color that comes to mind. See it filling the space of the sensation, whether it looks dark, bright, pale, or muted. Next, give it a shape. Does it feel jagged, smooth, round, stretched out, or shifting? Hold the image of this color and shape gently in your awareness.

With each breath, picture the color or shape slowly changing. Perhaps the edges begin to blur. Perhaps the color lightens or becomes more transparent. Maybe it shrinks in size or moves further from your body, creating more space. There is no right or wrong, only noticing what unfolds.

If the sensation resists changing, observe that as well. You might imagine softening its edges or surrounding it with a neutral border that helps contain it. Allow the image to shift in any way that brings a little more space or ease.

Continue to breathe as the color and shape transform. Notice how your body feels as this internal image evolves. You may sense more lightness, calm, or openness. Remain with this process for as long as it feels supportive.

When you are ready, let the color and shape fade from your awareness, as if the image gently dissolves into the air around you. Take one final steady breath, noticing how your body feels now. Then slowly bring yourself back to the present, opening your eyes when you are ready.

Exteroception (External)

I am allowed to fully experience the present moment. I can shift my awareness outside of myself with my five senses.

Exteroception refers to the sensory process by which we perceive external stimuli from our environment. It involves the five traditional senses: sight, hearing, smell, taste, and touch. Through exteroception, we detect and interpret information from the outside world, helping us navigate our surroundings, recognize potential threats, and engage in social interactions.

I am able to shift my awareness externally even as I notice my distress.

Grounding

Grounding is a technique used to help us stay present in the moment and reduce feelings of anxiety, dissociation, or distress. It involves bringing attention to the here and now by focusing on sensory experiences or specific aspects of the environment. Grounding techniques often utilize the five senses — sight, touch, hearing, smell, and taste — to anchor oneself in the present moment and create a sense of safety and stability. This can help you feel more centered, and connected to reality, especially during moments of heightened stress or overwhelm.

If external awareness feels awkward or distant at first, that's okay. Especially if you've learned to survive by tuning inward or staying hyperfocused on internal states, reconnecting with the outside world can feel unfamiliar. Start gently, with no pressure to feel anything specific right away.

Orienting to Present

Take a moment to find a comfortable position, sitting or lying down, and begin with a slow, deep breath. As you exhale, bring your attention to one of your hands resting in your lap or by your side. Let yourself settle into the sensation of being in the present moment.

Now, gently notice the shape and feel of your hand. Take a moment to recognize that this is your adult hand. You might observe the size, the texture of the skin, or even the lines that are unique to you. Let this awareness orient you to the present, reminding you that you are here, in this moment, and that this is your adult body.

Gently remind yourself that your adult hand shows you that you are no longer in a past experience, you are here now, as an adult, safe in this moment. As you continue to focus on your hand, notice how it feels to touch or hold it. Let this physical connection anchor you in the here and now.

This simple observation of your own hand can serve as a powerful reminder that you have grown, you are safe, and you can navigate the present moment with the strength of your adult self. Take a deep breath, allowing yourself to feel grounded in this awareness, and slowly bring your attention back to your surroundings when you're ready.

5-4-3-2-1: Returning to the Present with the Senses

The 5 things exercise is a practice of shifting your awareness from thoughts or body sensations, to experience the present moment, using the five senses.

Find a position that feels supportive, either sitting or standing. Let your body be held by the surface beneath you. Take a slow breath in, and as you exhale, begin to notice where your body makes contact with the world around you.

Begin with sight.

Notice five things you can see. Let your gaze move slowly. You might notice color, shape, light, or shadow. There is no need to search, simply let your eyes land on what is already here. As you look, notice if anything in your body shifts, even slightly.

Now bring your attention to touch.

Notice four things you can feel. This might be the weight of your body in the chair, your feet pressing into the floor, the texture of your clothing, or the temperature of the air on your skin. Stay here for a moment, allowing yourself to feel the steadiness of contact.

Gently shift to sound.

Notice three things you can hear. Sounds may be close or far away. You might hear something constant or something that comes and goes. Let the sounds move around you without needing to focus too hard.

Now bring awareness to scent.

Notice two things you can smell. If nothing stands out right away, that is okay. You might notice a subtle scent in the air or simply the absence of a strong smell.

Finally, bring attention to taste.

If you have something nearby and it feels helpful, you might take a small sip of a drink or a bite of food, noticing the flavor and texture as it moves through your mouth. If not, simply notice the natural taste in your mouth or the sensation of your breath as you exhale.

Take a moment to notice your body again. You might sense a small shift, or you may feel the same. Both are okay. This is not about changing your experience, but about creating space within it.

If it feels supportive, you can move through the senses again, or pause here, allowing yourself to rest in the present moment.

Mindfulness

When most people hear "mindfulness," they picture long meditations in quiet rooms. And while meditation is a beautiful practice, it can also feel intimidating or inaccessible at first.

Mindfulness, as we'll use it here, is about gently noticing the present moment, tuning in to what's around and within you without judgment. You do not have to clear your mind or do it perfectly. It is about coming back to now, over and over, in small ways.

You can practice mindfulness in simple, everyday moments. For example, when washing dishes, focus on the sensation of the water on your hands, the sound of the dishes clinking, and the texture of the soap. While taking a shower, notice the temperature of the water, the feeling of the steam, and the sound of the falling water hitting the floor. During a walk, observe your surroundings, the sound of your footsteps, the colors of the leaves, the feeling of the air on your skin.

Mindfulness can help when someone is stuck in their thoughts or overwhelmed by strong body sensations during distress or a trauma response. It reminds the body that the present moment is not the threat the mind and body perceive it to be. By focusing on the concrete aspects of the present, mindfulness reduces the influence of past experiences and future worries.

Mindfulness Practices

Mindful Handwashing

As you turn on the faucet, notice the sound of the water flowing and its temperature as it touches your hands. Feel the smoothness of the soap as you lather it between your fingers and palms. Pay attention to the sensation of the bubbles and the texture of your skin as you rub your hands together. If your mind begins to wander, gently bring your attention back to the feeling of the water and the soap. Focus on the rinsing, watching the soap wash away, and notice the clean, refreshed feeling of your hands afterward.

Mindful Walking

As you begin to walk, tune into the sensation of your feet touching the ground. Notice the rhythm of your steps, heel to toe. Feel the weight of your body shifting with each movement. If your mind drifts to other thoughts, acknowledge them, then gently return your focus to the physical sensations of walking. Listen to the sounds around you, feel the air on your skin, and continue walking, staying present with each step.

Mindful Eating

Take a small bite of food and pause before chewing. Notice its texture, its weight in your mouth, and any flavors starting to emerge. Slowly begin to chew, paying attention to how the taste changes and the sensations on your tongue. If your mind starts to wander, gently bring it back to the experience of eating: the textures, flavors, and sensations in your mouth. Continue to eat slowly, savoring each bite.

Moving Between External And Internal

This exercise supports your ability to move attention between your inner experience and the external world while maintaining a sense of steadiness and continuity. It can be adapted in many ways, but for this practice, you will choose one internal point of focus and one external point of focus and return to the same two places each time.

This practice is most supportive when you are within or near your window of tolerance. When the system feels flooded or collapsed, even gentle shifts of attention can feel like too much. Practicing in small, manageable moments helps build capacity gradually.

Exercise

Begin by finding a comfortable position, either sitting or lying down. Take a slow breath in, and as you exhale, allow your body to settle a little more into where you are. You do not need to relax completely. Simply become aware of the support beneath you.

Let your attention move inward to a single neutral sensation you will stay connected to throughout the exercise. This might be the points of contact where your body meets the surface beneath you, such as your back against the chair or your legs supported by the floor. Sense the weight of your body and the steadiness of that contact, allowing your awareness to rest here for a few moments without trying to change anything.

When you feel ready, gently let your attention move outward to one specific object in the room. Choose something simple and still. Take in its shape and how it exists in space. You might observe its edges, its size, or the way it relates to what surrounds it. Let your eyes settle here briefly.

Then allow your attention to move back to the same internal sensation. The contact beneath you is still here. You may sense the familiar pressure or support. If anything feels slightly different, simply let that be part of your experience.

When it feels comfortable, let your attention move outward again to the same object. This time, take in another aspect, perhaps its color or the way light falls across its surface. Let your gaze rest without effort.

After a few moments, allow your awareness to settle again into your internal anchor. There can be a sense of continuity here, of still being here, still supported, even as your focus shifts.

You can continue moving between the same internal sensation and the same external object at a pace that feels manageable. Over time, the movement itself may begin to feel smoother or more familiar.

If at any point this feels activating or overwhelming, you can pause and stay with the internal sensation until your system settles. There is no need to push beyond what feels supportive.

When you feel complete, take a slow breath and allow your awareness to widen back into the present moment. Sense the space around you and your body as you finish.

Practicing this gentle movement of attention helps strengthen your ability to stay connected to yourself while engaging with the outer world. Over time, it supports greater grounding, flexibility, and a sense of steadiness that you can return to when needed.

Detaching From Your Thoughts

When we are out of our window of tolerance, the thoughts believe it is their time to shine. Especially the negative ones. They come rushing out and demand attention. They can be intrusive and terribly pessimistic, rude even. Our bodies must be calmed, our emotions tended before we engage with them.

It may be hard to accept that thinking things isn't always useful. We may be very good at thinking things and solving problems. Thinking can also be a protective function, a need to solve for emotional safety. There is certainly a time and a place for thinking and solving, but it must come later, when our bodies are in our window of tolerance.

These exercises can be practiced outside or using videos of outdoor scenes. Being outside can increase grounding and connection to the present moment and is highly recommended.

Exercise 1

Go outside on a cloudy day and watch the clouds. Imagine sending your thoughts streaming from your head space out into the clouds. Would they be strings of letters? What would your thoughts look like? Watch them swirl around in the air, make shapes with them, as they move toward the clouds. Are they gently settled together in one spot, or are they scattered throughout? Are they moving or still? Visualize the thoughts slowly drifting away with the clouds.

Exercise 2

Go watch a stream or moving body of water. Spend some time watching the movement of the water, see how it shifts and ripples and dances. Listen to the sound if you can. Practice sending your thoughts into the water. Would they leap like fishes just above the surface? Would they reside under the foamy surface just skimming underneath? Or would they dive deep to the sandy bottom? Imagine them moving easily with the movement of the water, passing by and then away for now.

We may feel discomfort or even distress as we begin to notice how often we are outside our window of tolerance or how rarely we've paused to notice what's happening within us at all. Sometimes, it's not until we stop that we realize how long we've been elsewhere.

It is human to build upon what came before, to sort and label and reduce, until we can barely see the moment right in front of us. It is human to think and think and think. Thinking has its place, but it's not always where we need to be.

So here, we remember, wherever you are right now, you are okay. You are worthy and enough, just as you are. Nothing has changed, you are simply noticing, and that noticing is the beginning.

Take a breath here. A pause. A quiet check-in: *Am I in my window of tolerance?*

Containment

When working through trauma or difficult emotions, it's important to have ways to manage overwhelming feelings that arise. The safe holding place exercise can be used to set aside thoughts or emotions that feel too intense in the moment, allowing you to remain in control and can be practiced anytime to help manage emotional distress.

Unlike shut down, containing specific parts of our experience is an active choice to decide what we prefer and are capable of experiencing in the present moment. Practice setting emotions, thoughts, and sensations away can allow us to take charge of our experiences.

Safe Holding Place Exercise

Take a moment to get comfortable in your chair or on the surface supporting you. Let your breath come naturally, and allow your body to soften a little more with each exhale.

Before moving further, bring your attention to where your body is supported right now. You might notice the weight of your body in the chair, your feet resting on the ground, or the contact of your back against what holds you. Stay here for a few moments, allowing yourself to feel that support.

Now, gently bring to mind anything that feels too heavy, too sharp, or simply too much to carry right now. It might be a strong sensation, an emotion, a thought, or even a memory. Let it come into awareness in a way that feels manageable, without needing to push it away or hold on tightly.

As you sense it, notice where it lives in your body. You might feel it in your chest, your stomach, your shoulders, or somewhere else. There is no need to change it, only to recognize its presence.

Imagine creating a place where these difficult pieces can be set down for a while. It could take any form that feels right to you such as a strong chest, a wooden box, a clay jar, or something entirely your own. Picture it clearly, noticing its size, color, and shape. Let it be sturdy, and also responsive, able to hold what you place inside in a way that feels contained and secure.

When you are ready, begin placing what feels overwhelming into this space. You might imagine gently lifting it out of your body and setting it inside, or allowing it to move on its own into the container. Take your time.

As each piece is placed inside, notice what happens in your body. There may be a sense of space, a slight lightness, or a shift in pressure. You may feel very little change at all. Whatever you notice is enough.

Once everything that feels manageable has been placed inside, imagine closing the container in a way that feels secure. You might lock it, tie it, or seal it in a way that fits for you. Sense the feeling of it being held, not gone, but safely contained.

Choose a resting place for your container. It might sit on a high shelf, in a quiet room, beneath the ocean, far out in space, or in an entirely imagined place that feels safe. As you place it there, notice the sense of distance. You might feel it as space in your body, a quieting, or a softening.

Take a breath, feeling into your body again. Notice what is here now. There may be more room inside, or a small sense of ease. Allow yourself to rest in that, even if it is subtle.

This is not about getting rid of what you carry. It is about choosing when and how to be with it.

When it feels right to you, let your awareness return to the room around you. Feel the support beneath you again, hear the sounds around you, and gently open your eyes.

Carry with you the sense that this holding place remains available, something you can return to whenever you need space.

End-Of-Chapter Practice: Awareness In Motion

This week, continue noticing the shifts in your body, the gentle rises, the dips, the movement toward or away from presence. As you do, begin to explore how your awareness moves with it.

You've been practicing neuroception all along, your system scanning for cues of safety or danger. Now, deepen that practice by noticing where your attention lands and gently guiding it between different places.

You might ask yourself:

Am I noticing something inside (interoception)?

Am I noticing something outside (exteroception)?

Am I caught in a thought?

Practice gently shifting your awareness between these states. Try a few of the exercises in this chapter, even just one. Let your body lead. Feel your breath. Then listen to a sound. Then return to a thought. Notice how your body responds as your focus moves.

There's no right order, no preferred state, only a growing capacity to notice and choose. This is your awareness in motion.

You might also reflect:

Where does my awareness go most easily?

What is harder to stay with: thoughts, sensations, or the world around me?

When I shift my attention, how does my body respond?

What helps me return when I feel pulled too far in one direction?

Each shift you make, even the smallest one, is a new connection. Each moment you notice is a moment of choice. You're doing it. Keep going.

Identify the emotion

Objective: Understand the felt experience and message of the core emotions.

Your entire life only happens in this moment. – Eckhart Tolle

Out beyond ideas of wrongdoing and rightdoing,

There is a

field. I'll meet you there.

When the soul lies down in that grass,

The world is too full to talk about.

Ideas, language, even the phrase each other

Doesn't make any sense. – Rumi

But feelings can't be ignored, no matter how unjust or ungrateful they seem. – Anne Frank, The Diary of a Young Girl

By now, you may have noticed shifts in your body, tension rising, muscles relaxing, breath catching or deepening. You've practiced tuning in, gently observing your internal world and shifting between these states. And naturally, a question might arise: *How do emotions play into all of this?*

When the body speaks through sensation, the emotions are often not far behind.

Before emotions have names, they live first as physical sensations: tightness, fluttering, stillness, warmth, collapse. It's normal for feelings to exist in the body before we can find words for them.

Emotions are not just ideas in the mind. They are embodied experiences with physiological and sensory components, and greatly shaped by our personal history. They help us respond to what is happening around and within us. In the same way that your body detects threat or safety without conscious thought, your emotions are often developing and underway before you even realize it.

We'll explore what each emotion feels like in the body, how it relates to your nervous system state, and what it might be trying to communicate. There is no pressure to get it "right." There is only the invitation to notice. Just like before, your job is not to fix, only to become familiar.

The Emotions

Emotions

Emotions are mental states brought on by neurophysiological changes, associated with thoughts, feelings, behavioral responses, and a degree of pleasure or displeasure. There is no scientific consensus on a definition.

Feelings

According to the APA Dictionary of Psychology (an authoritative reference published by the American Psychological Association, defining over 25,000 terms in psychology and related fields), feelings are "subjective, evaluative, and independent of the sensations, thoughts, or images evoking them."

An emotional state or reaction.

And my personal favorite.

a belief, especially a vague or irrational one.

Feelings and emotions are neither right nor wrong, good or bad. They are a natural part of human experience. Healing involves embracing and gently tending to each of them. They provide information about our needs, boundaries, likes, and dislikes while focusing our attention.

Exercise

You may have heard people say the phrases below. What emotion do you think they're conveying to you with these described sensations?

I nearly jumped out of my skin.

I broke out in a cold sweat.

It made my skin crawl.

I was heated!

I had a lump in my throat.

I was grinning from ear to ear.

Through the practices in Chapters 1 and 2, you may have noticed sensations in your body and gained insight into your current state. Or perhaps not. There is no right or wrong, no goal to achieve. You are worthy and safe exactly as you are right now.

If you are feeling a sense of disconnect from your physical experience, know you're not alone, more people are experiencing this disconnect than not in recent years. You might be resistant to processing the sensations you are feeling. Remember, disconnection and numbness are sensations too. Our purpose here is to gently bring awareness to whatever you're experiencing right now.

It's important to remember that numbness, blankness, or a sense of shutdown are not the absence of emotion, but part of how the body responds to overwhelm (when emotions feel too intense or come on too fast). These, too, are valid emotional body states, worthy of noticing and compassion.

It is up to you to determine your tolerance level for exploring this feeling of disconnect from physical sensation. Shutdown often needs an increased feeling of safety in the body for us to allow in the physical sensations we are experiencing. The same is true with heightened fight or flight responses.

I recommend starting with increasing your felt sense of safety in the body and learning to respond to the physical sensations of fear and the emotional needs of fear. This will be explored further in chapters 6 and 7. A therapist can also help guide you through this practice and assist in establishing an increased feeling of safety. Once you have established a firm anchor of safety within yourself, begin with awareness, though I suspect it will already be there.

If you have already noticed something, perhaps something in your body, just sit with the sensation for a while.

Formation Of Emotions

Let's direct our attention back to our newly formed self. We are a little older now, learning more about the world and strategies beyond crying.

Do you see us there around 2 months of age? We begin smiling and quickly learn this gets the attention of our caregivers and we smile more. Enjoyment soon follows with smiles and laughter at the antics of our caregivers and sheer pleasure at the world around us.

A side note about surprise: When something surprises a baby, like an object not behaving the way they expect it to, they not only focus on that object but ultimately learn more about it than from a similar yet predictable object. The surprise of a new object, experience, or response increases attention, and the chances for our brain to highlight it on our mental map.

The other emotions are not far behind with unpleasant sensations turning more specific to things like disgust, fear, sadness or anger. At 6–8 months of age, a newly formed human feels mad when thwarted from a goal, sad when unable to access their caregiver, and fear when meeting a stranger.

From the moment we enter the world, we begin learning its ways and rules through our interactions. Our caregivers play a pivotal role in this process, naming and responding to our sensations, teaching us what they mean as they feed, hold, pat, change, smile at, sing to, rock, and bathe us. These early responses shape our understanding of self, others, and the world, embedding deep emotional learnings within us.

The framing and responses we receive are heavily influenced by our caregivers' own emotional understandings, the beliefs they carry about emotions, shaped by their life experiences and upbringing. How caregivers view and respond to emotions—whether with acceptance or dismissal, warmth or indifference—lays the groundwork for our emotional experiences, responses to those emotions, and beliefs about them.

Did you have a physical response to thinking about how our newly formed self learns about emotions? Can you identify that emotion? Did you push the emotion away or allow yourself to feel it and tend to it?

If you find the sensations or emotions that arise feel overwhelming, it's okay to pause and return to grounding practices from earlier chapters. There is no race. Moving between awareness and regulation builds trust in your system over time.

The Six Core Emotions

Six Core Emotions

According to Paul Ekman's theory of emotions, there are six core emotions including fear, sadness, anger, disgust, surprise and enjoyment/ happiness.

Emotional State

Refers to the moment-to-moment internal experience, shaped not only by how we are thinking about what is happening, but by how our body is responding to it. It includes shifts in sensation, nervous system activation, and felt sense, and is influenced by past experiences and the beliefs we have formed about ourselves, others and the world.

Emotions are a process, a particular kind of automatic appraisal influenced by our evolutionary and personal past, in which we sense that something important to our welfare is occurring, and a set of psychological changes and emotional behaviors begins to deal with the situation. – Paul Ekman, PhD

Emotions exist on a spectrum and are subjective.

As you read through the core emotions, connect any physical sensations you have noticed in your own body to the related emotions. Notice any beliefs or meaning-making (positive, negative or neutral) that come up related to the core emotions and set aside for later.

Fear

Fear is an unpleasant emotional state that arises when something is perceived as threatening or likely to cause harm. It is a rapid, body-based response shaped by both present experience and past learning, organizing the body for protection through escape, avoidance, or stillness. Fear can emerge quickly after surprise and may alternate with anger as the body responds to what feels threatening.

It can feel like butterflies in the stomach, a racing heart, tightness in the chest, a surge of energy, or a pull toward freezing or shutting down. You might notice heightened alertness or, at times, fog or disconnection. How does fear feel in your body?

Why Humans Feel Fear (Triggers)

Fear is triggered by situations or stimuli that signal potential harm or danger. These triggers can be external, such as encountering a wild animal or hearing a sudden loud noise, or internal, such as thoughts or memories of past traumatic events. Fear is a universal emotion, recognized across cultures, and is crucial for survival. Fear can be triggered by both immediate physical threats and more abstract concerns, such as emotional safety, fear of failure, or fear of the unknown.

How Fear Feels in the Body

Fear moves through the body like a current, charged and alive, pulling every sense toward alertness. The heartbeat quickens, breathing turns shallow, and adrenaline surges, preparing the body to move. Muscles tighten, especially through the arms and legs, ready to strike or run. A chill or flutter ripples through the stomach as blood shifts from the core to the limbs. Vision narrows, hearing sharpens, and the mind locks onto the source of danger with fierce precision. This is fear in hyperarousal, the body bracing for survival. When it endures too long, it drains the system, leaving behind trembling exhaustion and unease.

Fear can also quiet the body instead of charging it. When escape feels impossible, the system folds inward, slipping into hypoarousal. Muscles lose strength, breathing slows, and energy sinks low. Cold gathers in the hands and feet as blood retreats to the center. The world feels distant, movements slow, and the mind clouds in a fog. This is the freeze of fear, a stillness meant to conserve energy and protect.

Whether it surges into movement or collapses into stillness, fear reshapes the body around safety. Each reaction is the nervous system's way of guarding life, a wordless instinct to survive.

Window of Tolerance

When fear arises within the window of tolerance, it serves as an adaptive signal, heightening awareness without overwhelming the system. The heartbeat may quicken, and alertness may sharpen, yet these sensations remain manageable, allowing for clear thinking and deliberate action. In this state, fear enhances focus and strengthens protective instincts, transforming from a reactive force into a steady guide.

Within the window of tolerance, fear serves as a source of clarity and vigilance rather than tipping the body into hyperarousal or hypoarousal. Instead of spiraling into distress, the body remains engaged, responsive, and capable of navigating challenges with strength and precision.

Sadness

Sadness is an emotional state of unhappiness, ranging in intensity from mild to extreme and usually aroused by the loss of something or someone highly valued or an unmet longing. It is a bodily message telling us what has been lost and what we need. Sadness often exists alongside other emotions, including anger when we feel abandoned, fear when we wonder how we will cope or move forward, and even moments of joy when remembering something meaningful or feeling comforted by others. It can feel heavy, slow, achy, painful, tired, hollow, empty, drained, numb, disconnected, or restricted. How does sadness feel in your body?

Why Humans Feel Sadness (Triggers)

Individuals experience sadness as a natural and adaptive response to loss, whether it's the loss of a loved one, a relationship, an opportunity, or a personal dream. Sadness can also be triggered by unmet expectations, feelings of rejection, or being a witness to suffering in others. From an evolutionary perspective, sadness encourages us to slow down and reflect, conserving energy while we process what has happened. It often signals to others that we need support, fostering empathy and social bonding.

How Sadness Feels in the Body

Sadness often settles in the body as a heavy, sinking sensation, weighing down the chest, shoulders, and face. Muscles may tense or grow fatigued, leading to a drooped posture and a sense of exhaustion. Breathing becomes shallow and irregular, reinforcing a feeling of constriction or lethargy. The face naturally reflects the emotion, a downturned mouth, furrowed brows, tear-filled eyes. Some may feel a lump in the throat, tightness in the chest, or an emptiness in the stomach, something vital may feel missing. These sensations not only mirror sadness but deepen its presence, anchoring the emotion in the body.

When sadness becomes overwhelming, it can pull the body into hypoarousal. Energy drains away, leaving behind a sluggish heaviness, slowed movement, and a foggy mind. The world feels distant, engagement requires effort, and emotions flatten into numbness, a protective retreat from the weight of sorrow.

At times, sadness may push the body into hyperarousal, especially when entangled with helplessness or fear. Restlessness stirs, breathing quickens, and the heart races. This tension reflects the struggle between feeling sadness fully and resisting its pull.

Window of Tolerance

When sadness is experienced within the window of tolerance, it feels manageable. The body may carry a sense of heaviness in the chest or a lump in the throat, but there's space to process and express these feelings. In this state, individuals can reflect, grieve, and seek support, allowing sadness to serve its role in healing and adaptation without overwhelming the system.

Anger

Anger is an emotional state that arises when something feels interfering, unjust, or harmful. It emerges when a boundary has been crossed, a value violated, or an action feels wrong. Anger is a protective signal from the body, alerting us that something is important to us and that a response may be needed. Anger mobilizes energy. It prepares the nervous system for action, not necessarily aggression, but movement, protection, or change. Rather than telling us what is wrong with us, anger tells us what is not acceptable or sustainable. Anger can move alongside other emotions, including fear of causing harm to ourselves or others and disgust toward what blocks our path.

In the body, anger may feel hot, tight, buzzy, or coiled. It can show up as clenched jaws or fists, pressure in the chest, a pounding or racing heart, shallow breath, sweating, shaking, or a sense of energy building and needing release. For some, anger feels explosive. For others, it feels contained or pent up, like tension held just beneath the surface. How does anger show up in your body?

Why Humans Feel Anger (Triggers)

Humans feel anger as a natural response to situations where they perceive a threat, unfair treatment, or a barrier. Triggers for anger can include personal slights, unmet expectations, perceived injustices, or physical threats to self or loved ones. Anger is often a reaction to situations where we feel powerless or disrespected, and it can serve as a motivating force to take action or assert boundaries.

Anger can also show up defensively in protection of another emotion like sadness or fear. If your anger feels like a reaction to feeling hurt, powerless, or exposed, it could be defensive anger, serving as a way to avoid those underlying emotions. *Is my anger coming from a place of defending myself from a real violation, or is it guarding a vulnerability I may not want to face?* Recognizing which type of anger you're experiencing can provide clarity and help guide how you respond to and process it.

How Anger Feels in the Body

Anger builds as heat beneath the skin, a rising current that demands release. Muscles tighten through the chest, arms, and jaw. The shoulders lift, fists curl, and breath grows shallow as energy gathers for movement. The heart beats harder, blood surges, and warmth spreads through the face and neck until it feels like the body itself is burning to speak or act. It is the body's way of saying no, of drawing a line where something has gone too far.

In hyperarousal, anger sharpens. The pulse races, breath quickens, and the body braces for confrontation. Urgency increases. Focus narrows, ready to defend or fight. While this surge can be protective, staying in it too long can leave the system overstimulated, thoughts blurred by the force of emotion.

Sometimes anger collapses instead of rising. When it feels unsafe to express anger or too intense to bear, energy drains away and the body shifts toward hypoarousal. Muscles loosen, heaviness sets in, and movement slows. The fire dims to embers of numbness or fatigue, the body's way of retreating from what feels unmanageable.

Anger is the body's movement toward protection, a surge of energy that can burn outward or fade inward, always reminding us that something is significant to us.

Window of Tolerance

When anger is experienced within the window of tolerance, it serves as a constructive force. The body might feel a surge of energy, a steady, purposeful tension in the chest or arms, while the mind remains clear and focused. In this state, anger can drive assertive actions, boundary-setting, and problem-solving without escalating into reactivity or overwhelm.

Contempt

You may notice that some emotion researchers now include Paul Ekman's later addition of *contempt* as a core emotion. Ekman originally identified six universal facial expressions: anger, fear, sadness, disgust, surprise, and enjoyment. In the 1990s, he proposed that contempt also has a distinct, recognizable expression, often marked by a one-sided lift of the lip.

Contempt is not explored in depth in this book because the framework here is organized around the original six core emotions. However, it can be helpful to briefly understand its function.

Contempt often carries a sense of moral judgment or perceived superiority. It may arise when someone feels that a value has been violated or that another person is acting in a way that feels beneath consideration. In the body, you may experience tightening in the jaw, asymmetry in the face, a pulling back through the torso, or a subtle turning away. There may be activation, but it is frequently paired with emotional distance.

From a nervous system perspective, contempt can function as a protective strategy. Where anger moves toward, contempt pulls back. Where anger says, "This is not okay," contempt says, "You are not worth my engagement." In some developmental contexts, especially when direct anger felt unsafe or punished, contempt may become a more socially permissible way to create distance.

Like the other emotions, contempt is not inherently good or bad. It is information. It may signal deeply held values, unresolved hurt, or protective distancing. If you notice contempt in yourself, you might gently ask: *What feels threatened? What boundary feels crossed? What part of me learned that distance was safer than direct expression?*

For the purposes of this book, we will return our primary focus to the six core emotions, while recognizing that emotional life is complex and continues to evolve as research develops.

Disgust

Disgust is an emotional state of aversion toward something offensive, a bodily message that something is toxic, literally or figuratively, to our well-being. It can feel clammy and repulsed, with nausea, an extreme urge to turn away, or a desire to hunch over. How does disgust feel in your body?

Why Humans Feel Disgust (Triggers)

Disgust is an evolutionary response that has developed to protect us from harm. Its primary function is to help us avoid things that might be dangerous, unhealthy, or damaging to our social cohesion. Common triggers of disgust include:

Food-related disgust: Spoiled food, unpleasant odors, or anything that might signal contamination or disease.

Bodily fluids: Bodily fluids are often sources of disgust due to their association with contamination and disease.

Moral disgust: Acts that violate societal norms, such as cruelty, betrayal, or injustice, can evoke a sense of moral disgust, which helps reinforce social and cultural standards.

Animal-related disgust: Insects, rodents, or other creatures that might be associated with filth or disease can also trigger disgust.

How Disgust Feels in the Body

Disgust triggers a visceral reaction, including nausea, a sick feeling in the stomach, or the urge to gag. Muscles tighten in the face, neck, and abdomen as the body braces against something harmful. The body instinctively recoils, creating distance. The face contorts as the nose wrinkles, the brow furrows, and the upper lip curls, signaling disgust to others.

When disgust surges suddenly, it can push the body into hyperarousal. A jolt of energy courses through the system, bringing a racing heart, nausea, or an urgent need to escape. The body tenses, primed to recoil or expel what feels offensive. In this heightened state, the intensity of disgust can be overwhelming, making it difficult to process or regulate.

If disgust becomes too overpowering, the body may shift into hypoarousal. Energy collapses, leaving a sense of heaviness or even paralysis. The world feels distant, sensations dull, and nausea lingers, as the body retreats inward to protect itself.

A deeply physical emotion, disgust shapes the body's response with its intensity, driving it toward rejection, recoil, or shutdown.

Window of Tolerance

When disgust is experienced within the window of tolerance, it is manageable and serves as a protective signal, helping us identify and avoid harmful or undesirable stimuli. The body may react with sensations like a slight tightening in the stomach or a scrunching of the nose, but these responses remain within a tolerable range. In this state, disgust can guide decision-making and boundary-setting without overwhelming the individual.

Surprise

Surprise is a brief emotional state due to unexpected events in the environment. It can be perceived as positive, negative, or neutral and is often quickly followed by another emotion, such as fear, amusement, relief, anger, or disgust, depending on how the event is understood. It is a bodily message that alerts us to something new or unexpected. It commonly involves a startle response and can feel like eyes widening, eyelids and eyebrows raising, jaw dropping, a rush of adrenaline, or a sudden jolt in the body. How does surprise feel in your body?

Why Humans Feel Surprise (Triggers)

Surprise occurs when something happens that deviates from our expectations or assumptions. This can be a sudden noise, an unexpected encounter, a surprising piece of news, or any event that is out of the ordinary. Evolutionarily, surprise is an adaptive response that prompts us to quickly assess new situations for potential threats or opportunities.

How Surprise Feels in the Body

Surprise moves through the body like a spark, sudden and bright, impossible to ignore. It brings a quick surge of energy that pauses movement and thought. The heart leaps, breath catches, and muscles tighten, especially around the face, neck, and shoulders. Eyes widen, the jaw slackens, and a tingling alertness spreads through the body, heightening awareness as it takes in what has changed.

When surprise is sharp, the body may tip into hyperarousal. The heart races, breathing quickens, and adrenaline floods the system, readying it to act. This burst can be protective in urgent moments, though it can also feel jarring or disorienting when the intensity lingers.

At times, a strong shock can have the opposite effect, pulling the body toward hypoarousal. Energy drops, awareness blurs, and a sense of numbness or distance settles in as the system struggles to process what just occurred.

Surprise is the body's instant recalibration, a sudden shift that can startle us into presence or, when too strong, stun us into withdrawal.

Window of Tolerance

When surprise is experienced within the window of tolerance, it can bring curiosity, excitement, or mild astonishment. The body might feel a brief jolt of energy, a quickened heartbeat or a sudden intake of breath, before settling into a state of balance. In this range, surprise becomes a moment of heightened awareness, encouraging adaptability and openness to new experiences.

Enjoyment / Happiness

An emotional state of enjoyment, ranging in intensity from mild contentment to deep joy. It usually arises from meaningful connection, accomplishment, or the simple pleasures of the present moment. It draws us closer to what feels safe or satisfying. It can feel light, warm, tingly, expansive, shimmering, buzzing, glowing, energetic, relaxed, full, flowing, or open. How does enjoyment feel in your body?

A note on happiness: Ekman initially included happiness instead of enjoyment in the six core emotions. He made the shift from happiness to enjoyment to provide greater precision in understanding and categorizing emotional experiences. While "happiness" and "enjoyment" are often be used interchangeably, the distinction becomes important when considering the broader implications of these terms in psychological research.

Over time, "happiness" has come to be associated more with an overall sense of well-being or life satisfaction, equivalent to a general contentment with your life. But this isn't necessarily an emotion. In contrast, "enjoyment" refers to a particular emotional experience tied to a specific stimulus or situation, such as laughing at a joke or taking pleasure in an accomplishment. Can I be "happy" when I have suffered a significant loss? Perhaps not, but can I enjoy a good belly laugh while sharing a memory with another close other? I hope so.

For our purposes, enjoyment and happiness can be interchanged. Whatever feels best for you. Just remember that we're talking about the emotional experience, not an evaluation of your life.

Why Humans Feel Enjoyment

We feel enjoyment as a natural response to activities or experiences that meet our needs, desires, or expectations. Enjoyment arises from many sources, including social interactions, achievements, sensory pleasures (such as food or music), creative activities, and moments of relaxation or connection.

Enjoyment serves an important evolutionary function by reinforcing behaviors that contribute to survival and well-being. For example, we may feel enjoyment when we connect with others, eat a good meal, or engage in activities that align with our values and goals.

How Enjoyment Feels in the Body

Enjoyment often spreads through the body as a warm, expansive sensation, radiating through the chest, heart, and face. A sense of lightness replaces tension, muscles soften, especially in the face, neck, and shoulders. You may smile or laugh. Breathing deepens, becoming steady and rhythmic, reinforcing an overall sense of ease. Some may notice a tingling or shimmering sensation. The body might feel glowing with energy. These physical responses not only reflect enjoyment but also amplify it, creating a feedback loop that sustains the feeling.

In hyperarousal, enjoyment can feel unreachable, drowned out by restless energy, a racing heart, or shallow breath. For those who associate joy with unpredictability or risk, even positive experiences may trigger unease. If past moments of excitement were met with disappointment, criticism, or harm, the nervous system may learn to treat enjoyment as a threat. Rather than evoking calm, it sparks fight-or-flight, manifesting as restlessness, tension, or an underlying sense of something about to go wrong.

In hypoarousal, enjoyment may feel distant or muted, as if behind a barrier. The body, caught in a state of shutdown, struggles to access the energy needed for pleasure, leaving sensations dull, flat, or unreachable.

Window of Tolerance

Enjoyment is a hallmark of being within our window of tolerance. Within this window, our nervous system supports openness, curiosity, and engagement, allowing enjoyment to emerge naturally. Experiencing enjoyment regularly not only reinforces our time spent within the window of tolerance but can also expand its boundaries. Over time, this makes it easier to navigate stress and remain connected to positive experiences, even amidst challenges.

Connect with Learning

Imagine how each of the following experiences would feel in newly formed self's body and connect the related emotion.

A caregiver has popped their head around the corner unexpectedly and said peek-a-boo.

Our caregiver is holding us and singing to us.

Our caregiver will not allow us to put something in our mouth.

Our caregiver has fed us a food we do not like.

Our caregiver is busy with household tasks when we would prefer comfort from them.

A stranger is visiting the home and wants to hold you.

You are out on a walk with a caregiver, and a loud dog has jumped and barked behind a fence nearby.

As you consider these emotions and the related sensations, you may notice yourself connecting them to various body sensations you recently became aware of in yourself.

How Do I Apply This?

Take a moment to picture yourself as you are right now. Just observing, no judgment. Imagine it is morning, and as a morning person, you feel at ease in the rhythm of your routine. You're in the kitchen, getting coffee started and making pancakes. A close other, your partner, child, or friend, is there with you. They casually mention, *I'm getting breakfast with my buddies*, give you a quick hug, and head out the door.

Your brain registers this moment instantly, pulling from past experiences to make sense of it before you're even fully aware. A signal fires through your body, stirring something inside you. Quick, immediate, visceral. Before thoughts form, your body responds.

The Power of the Pause

This is where we pause.

Pausing in these moments can be difficult. Our brains move fast, often carrying us into thoughts or reactions before we even realize our internal state has shifted. But it's never too late to pause.

Right now, the why and the solving don't matter. Before we analyze or respond, we first regulate.

Whenever you do notice a shift, there is no judgment, only awareness. The moment of noticing is the invitation to turn inward.

In this scenario, your close other has already left, making it easier to pause. But in other situations, stepping away might be necessary. If so, communicating this need, when safe, can help establish healthier dynamics over time.

Bringing Awareness to the Body

The time it takes to identify what's happening in your body will vary based on your level of awareness. Some people feel every sensation intensely, others struggle to sense anything at all. Wherever you are in this process, you are doing well.

Let's return to the kitchen. There you are, having clearly felt something shift. You pause. Since you're in the early stages of this practice, you start by noticing the sensation that grabbed your attention. Then, you scan briefly and ask yourself what else is happening in my body?

If you need a guided scan, refer back to the brief body practice in Chapter 1.

Ask yourself:

What do I notice in my body?

Can I name the sensations?

What are they communicating to me?

Am I inside my window of tolerance or outside of it?

If outside, am I in hyperarousal or hypoarousal?

Scan as many times as needed, at your own pace. Maybe you feel a pit in your stomach, a buzzing sensation in your limbs, a racing heart, or a quickening breath.

Connecting Sensation to Emotion

Do you notice an emotion tied to these sensations? Can you name it?

As you explore, do you find yourself labeling the sensations as good or bad? Are any thoughts surfacing about what they mean? Gently acknowledge these thoughts, then invite them to step aside.

Now, think of the core emotions list. Do these sensations match with fear, sadness, anger? Perhaps your reaction is shaped by past experiences, associating the comment with rejection, abandonment, or unmet expectations.

There is no right or wrong answer, only increased insight. As you sit with this, remind yourself: You are safe. You are whole. You are exactly where you need to be. Notice what you are allowing and what you are pushing away.

Once we name the emotion, our instinct is often to jump into thinking about it, rationalizing, solving, analyzing. But for now, we stay with the body. We continue focusing on the felt sense of the emotion, letting it exist without rushing to change it.

This is where deeper awareness begins.

Secondary Emotions

Secondary emotions can offer a helpful entry point when identifying what is happening in the body. You may find it useful to reference a feelings or emotion wheel as a guide. Start with whatever emotion you can name, then gently trace it back toward a core emotion, as this is often where the body is organizing its response.

Each of the core emotions unfolds along a range. What we often label as separate emotional experiences are frequently different intensities or expressions of the same underlying state. As activation shifts, so does the way the emotion is felt, named, and expressed in the body.

Fear

Fear may begin as a subtle unease, often labeled as nervousness or anxiety, and build into dread as the body senses increasing threat. When options for safety feel limited, it can deepen into desperation. At higher levels, fear moves into panic, horror, or terror, where the nervous system is fully organized around survival. As it intensifies, fear may also give rise to overwhelm, helplessness, or irritability, especially when it begins to blend with anger.

Sadness

Sadness can start as disappointment or discouragement, a quiet sense that something did not unfold as hoped. As it deepens, it may become resignation or helplessness, and then move into hopelessness when the body no longer expects change. At its heaviest, sadness shows up as grief, despair, or anguish, often accompanied by a slowing, heaviness, or inward pull.

Anger

Anger often begins as irritation or annoyance and builds into frustration as tension increases. With more activation, it can shift into exasperation or defensiveness, where the urge to push back becomes stronger. When sustained or unresolved, it may take the form of bitterness or vengefulness. At its peak, anger becomes fury, with the body fully mobilized for action and release.

Disgust

Disgust may first appear as mild dislike, then strengthen into aversion as the body begins to pull away. As intensity increases, it becomes repugnance, and at higher levels, revulsion or loathing, where rejection feels absolute. The body often responds through contraction or recoil, and disgust may overlap with anger or fear when something feels offensive or unsafe.

Surprise

Surprise moves differently than other core emotions. Rather than deepening along a spectrum, it acts as a rapid shift in attention, quickly organizing into another emotional state depending on how the experience is interpreted.

Enjoyment

Enjoyment may begin as simple sensory pleasure and expand into warmth, connection, or joy. As it deepens, it can take the form of amusement, relief, or contentment, and further into pride or shared meaning. At its fullest, enjoyment becomes excitement, wonder, or even ecstasy, often felt as openness, lightness, or increased energy in the body.

End Of Chapter Practice: Noticing And Naming The Emotion

This week, continue noticing the shifts in your body. As your system moves through moments of activation, settling, heaviness, or openness, gently turn your attention toward the physical sensations present.

Pause at least once a day, even when nothing feels urgent. Let this be a quiet check-in rather than a response to distress.

You might ask yourself:

What sensations am I aware of right now?

Where do I feel them most clearly?

Are they steady, pulsing, tight, warm, heavy, light?

Stay with the sensation first. Notice its texture, its temperature, its movement. Let your awareness rest there without trying to change it.

Then, gently wonder:

If this sensation had an emotion connected to it, what might it be?

Does it feel like anger, sadness, fear, disgust, surprise, or enjoyment?

Am I feeling the emotion in my body, or thinking about the emotion?

There is no need to be precise. Sometimes you will know immediately. Sometimes you will guess. Sometimes you will not know at all. The noticing is what makes a difference.

You might also observe:

Are there emotions that feel easier to name?

Are there emotions that move me outside my window of tolerance?

Do certain emotions pull me toward hyperarousal or toward shutdown?

If you find yourself analyzing, gently return to the body. If you feel uncertain, stay with the sensation. Let the emotion exist without needing to confirm it.

Over time, patterns may begin to emerge. Certain sensations may reliably connect to certain emotional states. Your body has likely been speaking this language for a long time. You are simply learning to listen more closely.

Each moment of noticing strengthens that connection. You are building fluency in your own internal world.

Keep going.

Acknowledge and validate

Objective: Learn to acknowledge and validate your emotional experience

Just like children, emotions heal when they are heard and validated. – Dr. Jill Bolte Taylor

When I'm overwhelmed, I force myself to do one simple thing before I have to make a decision; Close my eyes and take three deep breaths. Sometimes even three deep breaths can change everything. – Tracy McConnell, How I Met Your Mother

You do not have to be good.

You do not have to walk on your knees

For a hundred miles through the desert, repenting.

You only have to let the soft animal of your body

Love what it loves. – Mary Oliver, Poet

You've Identified Your Body Sensations And Related Emotions, Now What?

Now that you've begun identifying the emotions in your body, this chapter invites you to stay with them a little longer. Instead of analyzing or pushing them aside, we begin the practice of acknowledgment, of saying, *I see you.*

For many of us, emotions were ignored, minimized, or overwhelmed in early experiences. It can feel unfamiliar or even unsafe to meet them with care. But acknowledgment is the first step in building trust with yourself.

You are learning to become a safe place for your emotions to land.

We'll explore what it means to validate an emotional experience, not by fixing or justifying it, but by letting it exist. You don't need to agree with it or like it. You only need to witness it with honesty and gentleness. This is the beginning of emotional intimacy with yourself.

Acknowledge

To accept, admit, recognize something.

We begin by creating space for the emotions. Your emotions are just as much a part of you as are your thoughts and experiences.

It helps to begin by acknowledging your felt experience here in this present moment. Speak the core emotion out loud or acknowledge the identified emotion internally to yourself. Whatever feels most comfortable. We recognize our experience without judgment.

In acknowledgement lies acceptance of experience.

I am feeling angry.

I am feeling scared.

I am feeling sad.

I am feeling disgusted.

I was surprised and it scared me.

I was surprised and it made me feel angry.

I am feeling enjoyment.

In Irish, when you talk about emotion, you don't say, 'I am sad'. You'd say, 'sadness is on me' 'ta bron orm'.

"And I love that because there's an implication of not identifying yourself with the emotion fully. I am not sad, it's just that sadness is on me for awhile. Something else will be on me another time, and that's a good thing to recognize. – P.O. Tuama

There are a vast array of opinions around the language we use about self and self experience. I am scared versus I am feeling scared. While we do not want to identify self with our emotional experience, it helps to label the identified emotion with plain language at the beginning of these practices.

Breathing 101

Breathwork is included here because it is a skill people often know and already use. It can help increase our tolerance and help us respond in new ways to our experiences. Breathing at its best can ground us to the present and aid us through discomfort. If we have long responded to emotions by thinking them, pushing them down, arguing with them, or solving them, it can feel very uncomfortable, foreign, and sometimes even unsafe to acknowledge them.

Breathwork

Conscious, controlled breathing used to influence the body's emotional, mental, and physical state.

Breathwork is a tool commonly recommended to reduce anxiety, ground, and connect with your body. Breathwork can help with all of these things but during high levels of hyperarousal, breathwork can be more activating. Begin by practicing these exercises while in your window of tolerance, until you are more aware of your physical responses. Before assuming unpleasant physical sensations are related to emotions or nervous system dysregulation, please ensure you have a clean bill of health for your lungs and breathing.

Breathwork and Hyperarousal (Fight-or-Flight)

When we move into hyperarousal, marked by heightened alertness, fast breathing, and an overwhelming sense of urgency or fear, we've stepped outside our window of tolerance. In this state, the nervous system is revved up, making it hard to feel calm or think clearly. Breathing techniques that slow the breath, like diaphragmatic breathing or extending the exhale, can help bring us back toward the window of tolerance, calming the body and mind.

Breathwork and Hypoarousal (Shutdown/Freeze)

Hypoarousal is the opposite extreme, characterized by feeling numb, disconnected, or immobilized. Breathing becomes shallow and slow, mirroring the body's lack of engagement. Gentle, rhythmic breathwork can gradually awaken the system, nudging us back toward the window of tolerance and fostering a sense of safety and connection.

Breathwork and the Window of Tolerance

Breathwork practices such as balanced or coherent breathing help regulate the nervous system and keep us within the window of tolerance. Regular practice strengthens our capacity to return to this zone when stress pulls us into hyperarousal or hypoarousal.

Breathing Techniques For Nervous System Regulation

There are as many types of breathing exercises as there are opinions about breathing exercises. For our purposes, I will provide several that have worked best for me and references to others. I encourage you to explore and find what works best for you.

For Hyperarousal (Reducing Overactivation, Calming the Body)

The **Physiological Sigh** is a natural reflex for releasing stress and resetting the nervous system. To practice, take a deep inhale through your nose, filling your lungs almost completely. Without pausing, take a second, shorter inhale through your nose to fully expand your lungs. Then, exhale slowly and completely through your mouth, ensuring the exhale is longer than the inhales. Repeating this several times helps release excess carbon dioxide and signals the body to relax. This technique is effective for both hyperarousal and hypoarousal.

4-7-8 Breathing encourages deep relaxation by slowing the breath. Inhale quietly through your nose for a count of four, hold your breath for a count of seven, then exhale audibly through your mouth for a count of eight. Practicing this breath pattern for several rounds engages the parasympathetic nervous system, helping to slow the heart rate and promote a sense of calm.

Extended Exhale Breathing is another way to activate the body's natural relaxation response. Begin by inhaling through your nose for four counts, then exhale through your mouth for six to eight counts. Continuing this pattern for a few minutes stimulates the vagus nerve, reducing stress and bringing the nervous system into a calmer state.

Alternate Nostril Breathing (Nadi Shodhana) (Nadi Shodhana) is a traditional pranayama practice used to support balance and calm in the body and mind. To practice, gently close the right nostril with your thumb and inhale through the left nostril. Then close the left nostril with your ring finger and exhale through the right nostril. Inhale through the right nostril, switch, and exhale through the left. Continuing this alternating pattern for several rounds can help settle the nervous system and increase steadiness.

Nadi Shodhana, meaning "channel purification," comes from an ancient yogic tradition that describes breath as a way of influencing the flow of energy in the body. It has been practiced for thousands of years to support clarity, balance, and regulation.

For Hypoarousal (Increasing Energy, Engaging the System)

Box Breathing (Square Breathing) provides a structured rhythm to stabilize the breath and restore focus. To begin, inhale through your nose for four counts, hold the breath for four counts, exhale through your mouth for four counts, and hold again for four counts before repeating the cycle. This technique promotes a sense of alertness and balance. It may feel challenging during hyperarousal but can be grounding when experiencing disconnection or low energy.

Simple Breath: Inhale through your nose, imagining your breath traveling down to your pelvis and expanding gently in your lower belly. Pause briefly, then exhale through your mouth, letting the breath escape effortlessly, like a soft sigh. This steady rhythm supports nervous system regulation and presence.

Bell Jar Breath: Imagine your body as a glass dome slowly filling with air. As you inhale, the breath rises from the base of the body upward, expanding through the chest. As you exhale, it softens and releases from the top down. This visualization supports full-body awareness and a steady, controlled breath cycle.

Validate

Demonstrate or support the truth or value of.

Before we explore how to practice self-validation, it helps to first connect with the part of you who can offer it. The part who is steady, kind, and values your inner experience.

Think of this as beginning a relationship with your inner caregiver. This inner figure isn't perfect or all-knowing, but they are aligned with your values and capable of meeting your emotions with gentleness. They don't rush you to feel differently. They don't shame you for what you feel. They stay with the experience you are having now.

Before we validate, we'll pause, breathe, and practice being with ourselves the way a trustworthy caregiver would. Slowly, softly, and with compassion.

As you practice acknowledgment and validation, you're also strengthening your emotional tolerance, the foundation that will support you later when we begin working with thoughts and beliefs. Healing starts here, in the body, learning to stay present with what is, so that deeper change can unfold safely.

Practice: Creating an Inner Caregiver

This exercise is meant to help you connect with an internal presence who can offer support, steadiness, and care as you begin to validate your emotions. You don't need to force anything. Just allow the experience to unfold in a way that feels true to you.

Begin by settling into your body. Take a few slow, steady breaths. Inhale gently through your nose. Exhale with a soft sigh. Let your body feel held in the moment, no need to change anything. Just be here.

When you're ready, begin to imagine a part of you who can offer care, this will be your inner caregiver. This inner caregiver may look like you or not. It might have the qualities of someone you've trusted before, someone you've longed for, or someone who lives only in your imagination. Let the image come naturally.

What matters most is how this inner caregiver feels. They honor your truth without rushing to fix it, offering warmth without pressure and acceptance without conditions.

Ask yourself:

What would it feel like to be with someone who truly sees me and stays?

How does my body respond to the idea of someone being here with me, without needing me to change?

If I imagined this caregiver sitting beside me or placing a steady hand on my shoulder, what sensations arise?

Let yourself rest in this presence for a moment. Breathe with them. Let them stay with you.

There's no right way to do this. You might feel comfort, resistance, sadness, or even nothing at all. That's okay. You are still building trust. This caregiver is here for the long haul.

When you're ready, gently return to the room. Carry whatever pieces of that presence you can with you. You can return to them anytime. This is the part of you who will practice validation.

Reflect / Mirror

Determining the feeling or emotions in another person's verbal or body language, and reflecting those feelings back to the person.

Mirroring a child's emotions involves reflecting their feelings and expressions back to them, creating a sense of being seen, heard, and understood. By matching their tone, words, and body language, caregivers can validate a child's experience, fostering emotional safety and connection. This practice not only helps children develop emotional intelligence and empathy but also builds a foundation for open communication. Effective mirroring involves attentive listening, genuine acknowledgment of their feelings, and a mindful, nonjudgmental presence that reassures the child their emotions are valid and worthy of care.

Mirroring the six core emotions

Fear

Mirroring a child's fear involves acknowledging their feelings while providing reassurance and support.

Child: "The wind is blowing so hard. It's so loud!"

Caregiver (mirroring emotional response): "I understand, sweetie. Thunderstorms can be really loud and scary sometimes. But I'm here with you, and we're safe inside our home."

The caregiver mirrors the child's fear by acknowledging their emotions and expressing empathy. Additionally, the caregiver provides reassurance by emphasizing safety and their presence, helping the child feel comforted and supported during a frightening situation.

Sadness

Mirroring a child's sadness involves empathizing with their feelings and providing comfort and support.

Child: "I miss Grandma. I wish she was here."

Caregiver (mirroring emotional response): "I understand, sweetheart. It's hard when we miss someone we love. I miss Grandma too, and it's okay to feel sad about that. Would you like a hug?"

In this example, the caregiver mirrors the child's sadness by acknowledging their feelings and expressing empathy. By validating the child's emotions and providing reassurance, the caregiver helps the child feel understood and supported during moments of sadness.

Anger

Mirroring a child's anger involves acknowledging and validating their feelings while helping them understand and manage those emotions constructively.

Child: Makes growling noises. "My friend took my toy without asking!"

Caregiver (mirroring emotional response): "I understand, sweetie. It's really frustrating when someone takes something that belongs to you without asking. It's okay to feel angry about that."

The caregiver mirrors the child's anger by acknowledging and validating their feelings without dismissing, belittling them or trying to fix. By doing so, the caregiver helps the child feel heard and understood, which can ultimately help the child learn to manage their anger in a healthy way.

Disgust

Mirroring a child's disgust involves acknowledging their feelings while providing support and understanding.

Child: "Ew, this food looks gross! I don't want to eat it."

Caregiver (mirroring emotional response): "I see that you're feeling disgusted by the food. It's okay to have preferences and feelings about what you eat."

The caregiver mirrors the child's disgust by acknowledging their reaction to the food. Instead of dismissing or criticizing the child's response, the caregiver validates their feelings and offers reassurance. This approach helps the child feel heard and supported while also encouraging them to express their emotions openly.

Surprise (Pleasant)

Mirroring a child's surprise involves acknowledging their feelings and sharing in their sense of wonder or amazement.

Child: "Look! A butterfly landed on my finger!"

Caregiver (mirroring emotional response): "Wow, that's amazing! I see the butterfly on your finger. It must feel so special to have it land on you like that!"

In this example, the caregiver mirrors the child's surprise by expressing enthusiasm and sharing in the child's sense of wonder. By acknowledging the event and validating the child's excitement, the caregiver strengthens the emotional connection and encourages the child to continue sharing their experiences.

Surprise (Unpleasant)

Mirroring emotional responses to a child's scary surprise involves acknowledging their feelings of shock or fear while providing comfort and support.

*Child: *Screeches* "There's a spider in my room!"*

Caregiver (mirroring emotional response): "Oh my, I see the spider. It must have been surprising to see it there! I'm here with you, and we'll take care of it together."

The parent mirrors the child's surprise and fear by acknowledging the presence of the spider and expressing empathy. By reassuring the child that they are not alone and offering to address the situation together, the caregiver helps the child feel supported and less frightened by the unexpected encounter.

Enjoyment

Mirroring enjoyment to a child involves reflecting and affirming their positive emotions, thereby validating their experiences.

Child: "Look, I built a tower with my blocks!"

Caregiver (mirroring happiness): "Wow, that's amazing, sweetie! You did such a fantastic job building that tower! I can see how proud you are of your creation. It looks so tall and sturdy. Great work! You must feel so happy."

In this example, the caregiver mirrors the child's happiness by expressing enthusiasm, admiration, and validation for their accomplishment. By doing so, the caregiver reinforces the child's positive emotions and boosts their self-esteem, fostering a sense of joy and confidence in their abilities.

Ideally, we learn to mirror and reflect back our own emotions. Which of these strategies can you use to validate your own emotions?

Self-Validation

Self-validation begins with actively listening to yourself. Notice the felt experience of the emotion and allow it to be present, without needing to fix or judge it. Gently practice accepting how things are right now. Take time each day to tend to your emotional experience, creating space to listen to yourself.

Normalize the experience of your emotions and the related sensations in your body. Offer reassurance to yourself that your emotions are valid, acceptable and normal. Acknowledge that it's normal to have a range of emotions, even if they are uncomfortable. There is no other way you should be feeling, other than the way you are feeling, right now, in this present moment.It's normal to feel stressed about this.

It's okay to be sad about this loss.

It is okay to feel this way.

Anyone in my situation would feel this way.

There are no right or wrong emotions, only the emotion that I am experiencing.

Our early caregivers label these state changes for us. They acknowledge, name, connect behaviors and experiences to validate, mirror and normalize self's experience of the world and the related emotions. This teaches us to learn to tolerate emotional experiences and allow emotions to move through the body and on to a preferred or different emotional experience.

Other Aspects of Validation

Affirmations and positive self-talk aren't meant to replace feeling, they are meant to support the body and mind together. They offer gentle language to the nervous system and the thinking mind, reinforcing the safety and worthiness you are beginning to experience directly.

Affirmations and positive self talk are good tools to practice validating our experience.

Apply affirmations and self talk in the order you find most helpful. Some people may need affirmations of worth and value before being able to engage in positive self talk or vice versa. You are encouraged to find what works best for you and adjust the exercises to your needs. Sticking to the basic spirit of the exercise, of course.

Positive self talk and affirmations can feel fake, false, or forced at first. It is perhaps unfamiliar and very different from how you normally speak to yourself. Maybe you do not believe these statements. The subconscious mind may be used to punishing, deriding, fixing, or pushing away our emotional experience. You may have noticed some of these come up for you in the work of the previous chapters.

It may be painful to acknowledge these internal voices that argue with affirmations, but it also informs us. It is a chance to decide how we would like to respond to emotions in the future and choose a new way. It is never too late. We acknowledge and accept any increased awareness with curiosity and kindness.

The new way requires practice and trying new things. We will remember our nervous system is well versed in reducing input in the same tired ways. It will likely be very stubborn at first, especially toward learnings established in childhood. Those are meant to last. It may cause discomfort to respond differently. Think of how you would respond to a child or a close other with the same emotion. Refer to the earlier caregiver responses to the emotions if it is helpful.

Our newly formed self remembers that new things require practice and curiosity, falling and getting up and trying again. Please set aside your skepticism for now and humor your feelings for just a little while longer with us.

It is safe here.

Affirmations Of Self

The curious paradox is that when I accept myself just as I am, then I can change. – Carl Rogers

Unconditional positive regard

The acceptance and support of a person regardless of what the person says or does.

Client-centered therapy teaches therapists to have unconditional positive regard for clients in order to create the best conditions for healing and growth. This means separating the behaviors from the person who displays the behaviors. Their essential worth as a human never changes.

We should cultivate the same unconditional positive regard for ourselves.

Affirmations ask us to remember our inherent value and worth as a human being regardless of other factors.

Note: As you practice unconditional positive regard, affirmations, and positive self-talk, you may notice negative beliefs arising. Simply observe them with curiosity for now. You can write them down if that feels helpful. We will explore thoughts in a later chapter.

Components of Affirmations

Affirmations are pre-constructed, positive statements meant to be repeated regularly to reinforce a belief or mindset. They are structured and proactive, often used to instill a desired quality or belief over time. An example would be, *I am confident and capable*, repeated daily to build self-esteem. Our mind when given new possibilities likes to follow them and can often begin seeing those traits in the world around it. Much like the frameworks and beliefs formed early in life.

Affirmations

Say each of these statements to yourself and sit with whatever comes up for a moment. Notice what comes up in your body. Focus your attention on any pleasant sensations you find. Breathe into those sensations and enjoy them for as long as feels good. Notice any discomfort or resistance with curiosity.

Self-Love and Acceptance

I am good enough just as I am.

I am worthy.

I love and accept myself unconditionally.

I am worthy of love and respect from myself and others.

Emotions

I welcome all of my emotions as they come and go.

I am in tune with my emotions and listen to what they tell me.

I allow myself to feel deeply and authentically.

My emotions are powerful guides.

I embrace the ebb and flow of my emotions with compassion.

I honor my emotions, knowing they contribute to my growth.

I am strong enough to experience my emotions fully.

I am at peace with all my emotions, knowing they are temporary.

I trust myself to navigate my emotions with wisdom and grace.

Every emotion I feel is a valid part of my human experience.

Fear

Fear is trying to keep me safe. I can listen without losing myself.

I can feel fear and still stay present in my body.

This sensation is a signal, not a failure.

I can let fear move through me at a pace I can tolerate.

I do not have to push fear away. I can meet it with steadiness.

Fear is allowed here, even when I do not understand it yet.

I can bring my attention back to my breath and stay with the part of me that feels afraid.

Feeling fear does not mean I am in danger. It means my body is alert and protecting me.

I can be curious about the message beneath this tension.

Fear does not have to run my life for me to honor its presence.

I can stay connected to myself while fear rises and falls.

Sadness

Sadness is allowed to be here without being rushed away.

I can let this feeling settle in my body without needing to fix it.

This heaviness is a sign that something mattered to me.

I can move slowly and still be okay.

Sadness does not make me weak. It shows the depth of my care.

I can sit with this ache and offer myself warmth.

My body knows how to grieve in its own rhythm.

It is safe to feel this without collapsing into it.

I can hold space for sadness and still remain connected to myself.

Letting sadness move through me creates room for healing.

Anger

Anger is showing me that something is important to me.

I can feel this heat without losing control.

This tension is a signal, not a threat.

I am allowed to protect my boundaries.

I can stay with this rising energy and listen to what it wants me to notice.

Anger does not make me dangerous. It makes me aware.

I can let this emotion move through my body without acting on it immediately.

Disgust

Disgust is my body's way of saying something feels unsafe for me.

I can notice this reaction without letting it take over.

This urge to pull away is a form of protection.

I am allowed to listen to what feels harmful or not aligned.

I can stay grounded while sensing this aversion.

Disgust can speak to me without deciding for me.

My body is trying to keep me safe, and I can honor that signal with care.

Surprise

This jolt is my body waking up to something unexpected.

I can let myself settle before deciding what comes next.

Surprise is temporary. I can ride the shift in my body.

I do not need to understand everything right away.

I can pause, orient, and move at my own pace.

My body knows how to return to steadiness.

Enjoyment

I am allowed to feel good in this moment.

Enjoyment does not erase my pain. Both can exist together.

My body can take in warmth without waiting for it to end.

I do not need to shrink my joy to feel safe.

This lightness is welcome here.

I can let myself stay in connection when something feels good.

It is safe to experience ease and pleasure in my body.

Confidence and Empowerment

I am capable of figuring things out.

I believe in my abilities and have confidence in myself.

I am capable of achieving anything I set my mind to.

I trust myself to make the right decisions for my life.

Resilience and Persistence

If I don't know the answer, I will find it.

I am strong and resilient, capable of overcoming any obstacle.

I persevere in the face of challenges, knowing they are opportunities for growth.

I trust in my ability to bounce back from setbacks stronger than before.

Compassion and Kindness

I am compassionate toward myself and others.

I am allowed to treat myself with kindness.

I radiate love and kindness, making a positive impact on those around me.

I forgive myself for past mistakes and release any guilt or shame.

Safety

I am safe and protected in this moment.

I create a safe and nurturing environment for myself wherever I go.

I take precautions to keep myself safe while also remaining open to new experiences.

I am able to keep myself safe.

Mindfulness and Presence

I am present, in this moment, fully engaged, and aware.

I let go of worries about the past and future, focusing on the present.

I embrace each moment with gratitude and mindfulness.

Personalize these affirmations so they align with your own beliefs and values. Preparing a few statements in advance helps when you're first learning to tend to your emotions. With practice, they become more natural and easier to create in the moment.

Affirmations and self talk may seem like the same thing but positive self-talk is more spontaneous and situation-specific, while affirmations are pre-set and intended for consistent practice.

Positive Self-Talk

We are often our own worst critics. We speak to ourselves internally or think thoughts toward ourselves that we would not say or think toward another. Positive self-talk asks us to reframe our internal dialogue from a place of unconditional positive regard for self. A place full of compassionate understanding.

If you struggle to visualize a different response, speak to yourself like Mr. Rogers, Steve Irwin, Ms. Rachel, LeVar Burton, or return to the inner caregiver you created earlier. If that causes you to cringe, ask yourself why? Do you not deserve kind regard for yourself? What does kind regard mean about you? Just notice what comes up.

Components of Positive Self-talk

Positive self-talk is the inner dialogue you use when an emotion rises in your body. You do not have to pretend to feel better or push away what is real. Instead, acknowledge what you feel, validate why your reaction makes sense, and mirror your emotion in a way that helps you feel seen and heard on the inside. Positive self-talk also includes a sense of agency, which reminds you that you still have options, and realistic hope, which lets you look ahead without demanding that you change how you feel. These pieces work together to help you stay connected to yourself as the emotion moves through.

Positive Self-talk Examples

General

Okay, I'm feeling something right now. This reaction makes sense. I can slow down for a second. I've gotten through moments like this before.

Something is coming up in my body. That's alright. I can give myself a bit of space to feel it. This won't stay this intense forever.

I don't love how I feel right now, but it's okay. I'm here with myself. I can take this one moment at a time.

Fear

I'm scared. My body jumped fast, and that makes sense. I can look around and take a breath. I've handled fear before. I can handle this.

My chest is tight and my stomach dropped. This is fear trying to protect me. I'm here with myself. This will make more sense once I calm down a bit.

Okay, this is fear talking. I understand why it showed up. I can take this one small step at a time. I'll find my footing again.

A note on safety: *these statements should not be used in moments of actual danger to yourself or others.*

Sadness

I'm feeling sad. This feeling has a reason. I can be gentle with myself. This won't feel this heavy forever.

This hurts. Of course I'm sad. I can sit with myself for a moment instead of rushing this away. I can take this one small step at a time.

I feel low today. That's understandable. I can move slower and take care of myself. This will shift eventually.

Anger

I'm really angry right now, and I get why. Let me pause so I don't react too quickly. I'll come back to this when I feel steadier.

This really set me off. Anyone would feel this way. I'm going to slow down for a moment. I'll figure out what to do once the heat settles.

Yeah, I'm angry. Something about this crossed a line. I don't have to act on it right this second. I can return to this when I'm clearer.

Disgust

Ugh, that hit me wrong. I can feel myself pulling back. That reaction makes sense. I can take a little space and sort this out later.

I feel disgust in my stomach and throat. Something feels off. I can listen without judging myself. This feeling will ease once I understand what I need.

Yeah, that didn't sit right with me. I can give myself distance if I need it.

I'll figure this out once the intensity settles.

Surprise

Whoa, that came out of nowhere. No wonder my body jumped. Let me steady myself for a second.

That startled me. I'm going to pause and catch up. This will make more sense in a moment.

I wasn't expecting that. My heart is racing, and that's okay. I'll sort this out once the jolt fades.

Enjoyment

This feels really good. I can let myself enjoy it without shrinking it. I can stay with this feeling for a bit.

I'm actually enjoying this. That's allowed. I can take this in at my own pace. Good moments count too.

There's a warmth here that feels nice. I can let myself have this without guilt. I'll let it linger as long as it wants to.

Remember, these statements are designed to help you navigate your emotions in a healthy and constructive manner. Embracing your emotions and responding to them with kindness and understanding can lead to greater emotional resilience and well-being.

End Of Chapter Practice: Turning Toward Yourself With Kindness

In this chapter, you have been practicing how to acknowledge an emotion and the experience of it. Validation is not about agreeing with an emotion or making it go away. It is about letting yourself know that what you feel is real and allowed. This practice is an invitation to respond to your own experience with the same care you might offer someone you trust.

Begin by settling into your body. Notice where you feel supported. Let your breath move naturally.

Bring to mind an emotion that has been present recently. Choose something that feels workable, not overwhelming.

Notice how this emotion shows up in your body. Where do you feel it? What lets you know it is here? Let what you notice be enough.

As you stay with the sensation, offer a gentle acknowledgment. You might say quietly to yourself, I notice this, or this is here right now.

Now imagine turning toward this part of you with kindness. You are not fixing it. You are keeping it company.

Notice what kind of words feel possible in this moment. Not words you should say, but words that feel believable and supportive. You might try one of the following, or your own version:

It makes sense that I feel this.

I am allowed to feel this.

I can be with myself while this is here.

I am not doing anything wrong by feeling this.

Say the words slowly, and notice what happens in your body as you do. Do they soften anything? Do they feel neutral? Do some feel truer than others? All of that is information.

You may notice resistance to offering yourself kindness. If so, acknowledge that too. This feels hard, or part of me doesn't believe this yet. Kindness includes honesty.

Take a moment to notice whether this emotion feels more tolerable when it is met with kind self-talk, even slightly. You are not measuring success. You are noticing.

If the experience becomes too intense, gently shift your attention to a neutral place in your body or to something around you that feels steady. Returning to safety is part of turning toward yourself kindly.

Before closing, place a hand somewhere on your body that feels supportive. Offer one final phrase that feels grounding in this moment, such as, *I am here with you,* or *you don't have to go through this alone.*

When you are ready, orient back to the room. Notice light, sound, or color. Carry with you the felt sense of having responded to yourself with care.

Allow and sit with your emotions

Objective: Increase ability to allow and tolerate experience of core emotions.

Self-acceptance does not mean self-admiration or even self-liking at every moment of our lives, but tolerance for all our emotions, including those that make us feel uncomfortable. – Gabor Mate

You calm your feeling just by being with it, like a mother tenderly holding her crying baby. – Thich Nhat Hanh

To greet sorrow today does not mean that sorrow will be there tomorrow. Happiness comes too, and grief, and tiredness, disappointment, surprise and energy. Chaos and fulfillment will be named as well as delight and despair. This is the truth of being here, wherever here is today. It may not be permanent but it is here. I will probably leave here, and I will probably return. To deny here is to harrow the heart. Hello to here. – Pádraig Ó Tuama

We have spent time strengthening our awareness of physical sensations, and learning to recognize the core emotions woven into those sensations. We have paused with anger, sadness, enjoyment, surprise, disgust, and fear, not trying to fix them, but meeting them as they are.

We have practiced validating our experience, offering ourselves positive affirmations and compassionate self-talk when emotions arise.

We have gently noticed the thoughts that surface alongside feeling, allowing them to float past without needing to capture or solve them.

Through it all, we have continued tending first to the body.

Now, we deepen the work. We turn toward the emotions themselves, not to analyze or change them, but simply to allow them. We learn to sit with what is felt.

Tolerating The Emotional Experience

The young self learns to understand the coming and going of the emotions they experience. The ebb and flow of *all* the emotions — from fear and tears after a bump on the head to laughter and hugs with a caregiver or immediate engagement in play.

Ideally we learn to accept these states of our emotions and the shifts between them as a normal part of experience and not something to push away.

We cannot bypass our felt experience and expect to be effective in our thinking, responses, and behaviors.

90 Seconds

When a person experiences an emotion, such as anger, sadness, or fear, the physiological response triggered by that emotion typically lasts for about 90 seconds.

This concept, coined the 90-second rule, was introduced by Dr. Jill Bolte Taylor, a neuroanatomist. Dr. Taylor suggests that beyond this 90-second window, if a person continues to feel the emotion, it's typically due to the individual's thoughts and interpretations of the initial trigger which will in turn prolong felt sensations and the emotion.

It is important to note that the 90-second rule is a simplification and doesn't necessarily apply to all emotional experiences or situations. Emotions can be complex and influenced by various factors, including individual differences, past experiences, and current circumstances. While the 90-second rule offers a useful perspective on emotional processing, it's not a strict rule but more a rule of thumb.

Tolerating 90 seconds is a good goal to strive for in allowing the felt sensations of our emotions. We may only be able to allow and feel them for 5 seconds, 10 seconds, or 30 seconds right now given our current window of tolerance. If so, we will observe and notice that.

Allowing = Not Struggling Against

I allow in the physical sensations of the emotion I am experiencing. Emotions move through me with ease.

First return yourself to the identified emotion in the body and return focus to the felt sensations. *How am I experiencing this emotion in my body?* Gently allow yourself to experience the felt sensations of the emotion.

The sensations may seem unpleasant, causing resistance and a desire to push away the felt experiences. Sometimes, you may even go into shutdown to avoid the feelings.

We will gently remind ourselves here of the fullness of the human emotional experience. Emotions come and go as we experience and interact with our environment. All emotions are useful to us.

I am experiencing the physical sensation of emotion. While I do not prefer these sensations, I know they will shift, change, and pass through me.

Self-Regulation And Soothing Strategies

It can be helpful to engage in self-soothing strategies when allowing yourself to experience difficult emotions.

Self-soothing skills are typically developed in early childhood through the internalization of comforting experiences. Our newly formed self learns to engage in healthy self-soothing when caregivers are not around for co-regulation.

We will speak more on co-regulation in Chapter 7.

Individuals who didn't naturally acquire these techniques can still learn them through intentional efforts.

Here are some strategies to try.

Chest Patting

Place the palm of your hand on your chest, just below the collarbone. Then, using a gentle and rhythmic motion, begin patting or rubbing the chest area. You can adjust the pressure and speed of the patting to suit your comfort level. This self-soothing gesture can provide comfort and reassurance. Take deep breaths as you pat your chest to enhance the calming effect.

Peter Levine's Somatic Self-hug

To perform this self-soothing technique, gently bring one arm across your body, reaching under the opposite armpit, and allow your hand to rest on your upper back or side. Then, use your other hand to grasp the shoulder of the arm that's across your body. Hold this position for a moment, focusing on the sensation of support and comfort it provides. This gesture mimics the sensation of being embraced and can help promote feelings of security and relaxation and be particularly helpful during moments of stress or anxiety.

Hand-to-heart Grounding

Begin by placing one hand gently on your chest and the other on your forehead. Take a moment to notice your breath, feeling the gentle rise and fall beneath your hands. After a few breaths, slowly move the hand on your forehead down to rest on your abdomen. As you continue breathing, notice the rhythm of your breath expanding into your chest and belly. This shift encourages deeper, more intentional breaths, helping to calm the nervous system and bring a sense of balance and ease.

Tapping

Tapping, sometimes called bilateral movement, can help promote relaxation and reduce feelings of stress or anxiety. It can help ground you in the present moment and provide a sense of comfort and stability. There are many great tapping apps to get started.

Thigh / Knee Tapping

Sit comfortably and gently tap one thigh with the palm of your hand, then switch to tapping the other thigh. Continue alternating between thighs in a rhythmic pattern.

Foot Tapping

Sit or stand and gently tap one foot on the floor, then switch to tapping the other foot. Alternate between feet in a rhythmic pattern.

Crossover Tapping

Cross your arms so that your hands are resting on your upper chest or shoulders. Then, gently tap your right shoulder with your left hand, and your left shoulder with your right hand, in a rhythmic and alternating motion.

Slow Movement

Engage in slow, deliberate movements such as walking slowly around your space or outside, performing gentle stretches, or making slow, flowing movements with your arms and body. This deliberate pace encourages mindfulness and relaxation, allowing you to connect with your body and surroundings in a soothing manner.

Experiment with each technique to find what works best for you.

Some people may encounter challenges with self-soothing, they may feel undeserving of these strategies, view self-soothing as shameful, or believe that others should be responsible for comforting them. Should any of these things arise in you, just notice and continue affirming, validating and soothing self.

What self soothing strategies do you already use? What strategies can you think of to use in the future?

Which sensations feel tolerable and which do not? We continue to affirm self and engage in positive self-talk while we allow and sit with our felt experience.

Skills In Action

Returning to the Kitchen

Let's return to the morning kitchen scene from Chapter 3.

You've already identified the emotion, fear. The sensations are clear: a pit in your stomach, buzzing in your limbs, quickened breath, a racing heart. The urge to act comes quickly, maybe to reach out to someone close, express displeasure, seek reassurance, or solve it outside of yourself.

Pause

Instead, you pause.

You breathe through the impulse, shifting focus inward. Back to the body, back to the felt experience of fear.

There will be time for solving, for expressing, for co-regulation later. But right now, you allow yourself to fully feel what is happening, without needing to justify or change it.

I am feeling scared.

Self-Soothing in the Moment

As the emotion moves through you, self-soothing becomes your gentle companion, not to erase the feeling, but to support you as you stay with it. Maybe you place a hand on your chest, offering light pressure. Maybe you breathe intentionally, slow and deep, creating a rhythm of safety.

I feel the pit in my stomach. The buzzing in my body. My breathing is fast, and my heart is racing. I feel scared, but in this present moment, I am safe.

The mind may resist. Thoughts surface: *I shouldn't feel this way. I'm overreacting.* Old strategies learned long ago to minimize discomfort rise to push away the feeling.

Instead of pushing away the emotion, you notice, validate, and return to your chosen path.

In the past, I learned to suppress my emotions. Now, I allow myself to feel. It is safe and normal to have emotions. They may be uncomfortable, but they will pass.

Holding Space for the Felt Sense

The mind may try to analyze, to assign meaning, to rationalize. For now, you simply observe. Any negative beliefs that arise are met with curiosity, not judgment.

You continue breathing, continue self-soothing.

I am worthy and enough, just as I am, in this moment.

Fear is a natural part of life, and I embrace it as an opportunity for growth.

I trust myself to move through fear with resilience and self-compassion.

I am safe in this moment.

Notice any shifts. Perhaps the intensity remains, or perhaps something softens, just slightly. The goal isn't to force a change, but to remain present with what is.

Take one small step toward your preferred response, knowing that each moment of allowing strengthens your ability to navigate emotions with intention.

All happy families are alike; each unhappy family is unhappy in its own way. – Leo Tolstoy, Anna Karenina

How Do We Learn About Emotions

In a newly formed self's world, caregivers respond to emotions dozens of times a day. Through these repeated moments, the body learns what to expect when fear, anger, sadness, disgust, surprise, or enjoyment arise. Caregivers soothe, mirror, redirect, ignore, fix, or punish emotional expression, quietly shaping how emotions are felt, interpreted, and expressed.

Very early in life, babies begin distinguishing emotional expressions and mimicking what they see. Long before language or logic develop, the nervous system learns through observation and repetition. Newly formed self is learning not only how to move through their own internal experience, but also how to read the emotional states of others.

Over time, these experiences form an emotional map. Some caregiver responses support safety and tolerance for emotional states. Others unintentionally teach that emotions are dangerous, overwhelming, inconvenient, or something to manage quickly.

This is where early emotional beliefs begin to take root.

You might think of it as a garden shaped by repetition and response. What was met with care tends to grow more freely. What was punished, rushed, or dismissed often twists itself into protective forms. Families develop many ways of responding to emotion, some supportive, some limiting, often both.

Tread lightly here. We are not revisiting every detail of what happened. We are noticing what we learned about emotions and how those lessons show up in our present-day responses.

Ideally, caregivers model that emotions are not something to fear. They hold space, offer support, and help newly formed self learn that emotional states rise, shift, and move through the body. Through this process, the nervous system learns that feelings can be experienced without losing safety or connection.

The examples that follow explore how different caregiver responses shape emotional learning, through the lens of the core emotions.

Depending on your own experiences, the examples that follow may stir memories or sensations. As you read, notice what happens in your body. Stay gentle with yourself.

Examples of Caregivers Modeling Emotions

Positive Examples

Fear

The caregiver acknowledges the child's fear of the dark or of unfamiliar situations and offers reassurance and support. They help the child confront their fears gradually, providing comfort and guidance as they navigate new experiences and environments.

Sadness

The caregiver shows empathy and understanding when the child is upset about something, such as a pet passing away or feeling left out by friends. By comforting the child and validating their emotions, the caregiver teaches the child that it's okay to express sadness and seek support.

Anger

The caregiver models healthy ways to manage anger by calmly addressing frustrating situations without resorting to aggression or violence. For example, they might explain to the child why hitting isn't appropriate when they're angry and instead demonstrate deep breathing or taking a break to cool down.

Disgust

The caregiver calmly explains to the child why it's important to wash their hands before eating and after using the restroom. They demonstrate good hygiene practices themselves and encourage the child to do the same, emphasizing the importance of staying clean and healthy.

Surprise

The caregiver plans a special surprise for the child's birthday, such as a small party or a favorite dessert. When the surprise is revealed, they share in the child's excitement and joy, reinforcing positive emotions associated with surprises and celebrations.

Enjoyment

The caregiver expresses genuine happiness and excitement when the child achieves a milestone, such as taking their first steps or mastering a new skill. This teaches the child to recognize and celebrate moments of happiness.

Negative Examples

The following examples may be hard to read. Notice any emotions you are experiencing. Practice breathing and self-soothing strategies as you read through each example.

Fear

The caregiver exaggerates their own fears or anxieties in front of the child, projecting a sense of helplessness or vulnerability. This can cause the child to internalize the caregiver's fears and develop anxieties or phobias of their own, hindering their ability to cope with challenges and uncertainty.

Sadness

The caregiver responds to the child's sadness with impatience or criticism, telling them to *toughen up* or *stop crying.* This might also look like not noticing the child's emotional experience. This invalidates the child's emotions and teaches them to suppress or ignore their feelings, which can result in difficulties with emotional regulation later in life.

Anger

The caregiver frequently loses control of their temper, shouting or using physical punishment when they're angry. This teaches the child that aggression is an acceptable way to deal with frustration, leading to potential behavioral issues and difficulty forming healthy relationships in the future. Caregivers may also minimize and encourage the child to push down, tolerate or ignore feelings of anger.

Disgust

The caregiver expresses disgust or contempt toward certain foods or people in front of the child, instilling prejudiced attitudes and reinforcing negative stereotypes. This can lead the child to develop biased beliefs and attitudes based on the caregiver's example. Caregivers may also cross the child's boundaries or not respect the child's needs and preferences.

Surprise

The caregiver reacts negatively to unexpected events or changes in plans, becoming visibly stressed or angry. This teaches the child to fear surprises and uncertainty rather than embracing them as opportunities for growth and excitement.

Enjoyment

The caregiver constantly dismisses the child's achievements or joyous moments, showing a lack of enthusiasm or interest. This can lead the child to feel unimportant or unrecognized, impacting their self-esteem and emotional development.

Whether negative or positive, the way the caregiver models and handles emotions plays a crucial role in shaping the child's emotional intelligence and overall well-being.

It is hard to imagine, maybe it brings up sadness or anger or fear, but we hold with compassion and the understanding we cannot do better without knowledge to do so. This applies to both self and others.

We must learn a new way.

The act of allowing and acknowledging experience with acceptance and without judgment can itself be a monumental change. With clarity and awareness of where we are starting from and what is happening now, we can begin moving in the direction we prefer instead.

Self-attunement Practice

This practice can be used when noticing a shift in the internal emotional experience.

You have noticed an internal emotional shift. First, breathe into your body. Let your breath meet the sensation instead of moving past it. Notice how this emotion is showing up physically, the tightness, the heat, the heaviness, the fluttering, the pull inward, or the urge to move outward. Whatever is here, meet it softly.

Gently turn toward this experience inside you. Let your attention rest on it with warmth, the way you might sit beside someone who is hurting or overwhelmed. There is no need to push it away or solve it. Stay close to the sensation and let it know you are here.

Ask the emotion and the part of your body holding it what it might need right now. Listen without forcing an answer. The need may be small. It may want slower breath, more space, a moment of stillness, a steadier posture, or a simple acknowledgment. You can offer these things at your own pace.

It is normal to feel emotions, even when they arrive unexpectedly or feel out of place. It is okay to feel what you are feeling.

Protective Responses

Protective responses to avoid feeling emotions are quite common, especially when past experiences have shown that feeling certain emotions led to harm, rejection, or neglect. This often happens when someone has faced trauma including relational, emotional neglect, or situations where expressing vulnerability wasn't safe. Over time, the mind learns to shut down or suppress certain feelings as a way to protect the person from further emotional pain. These protective mechanisms can take on a variety of forms.

Examples of Protective Responses

If caregivers respond negatively to a child's emotions, the child may develop protective responses that persist into adulthood, often in unpreferred ways. Here's how some of these patterns can play out.

Fear

The adult may develop chronic anxiety or phobias, mirroring the caregiver's exaggerated fears. They might avoid challenging situations, feel overwhelmed by uncertainty, or struggle to trust their own resilience. Protective responses could include constant worry, avoidance of new experiences, or seeking reassurance from others.

Sadness

The adult may suppress their sadness, believing it's weak or unacceptable to show vulnerability. They might struggle to reach out for help or express their emotions, fearing criticism or rejection. Emotional numbing, denial of sadness, or avoiding introspective moments are common protective responses.

Anger

As an adult, they may either become overly aggressive or completely avoid confrontations, believing anger leads to harm or punishment. They might struggle with boundary-setting, fearing that any expression of anger could lead to rejection or violence. Alternatively, they could bottle up frustration until it explodes or use passive-aggression to express anger indirectly.

Disgust

The person may develop strong aversions or prejudices toward people, situations, or groups that echo the caregiver's expressions of disgust. They might also experience internalized shame, feeling disgusted with themselves when they fail to meet certain standards, leading to low self-esteem and critical self-talk.

Surprise

As an adult, the person might become hypervigilant or anxious in response to uncertainty or sudden changes, fearing that surprises bring chaos or punishment. They may avoid spontaneity and seek control in all situations to maintain a sense of safety, even if this limits their personal growth or enjoyment of life.

Enjoyment

As an adult, the person may have trouble fully experiencing or expressing joy. They might dismiss their own achievements or downplay moments of happiness to avoid feeling rejected or unnoticed. This could manifest as self-sabotage, reluctance to celebrate successes, or guilt over feeling good when others aren't.

Ask yourself *how are these things showing up for me now? What protective devices am I using that I don't need now? How might this response I have noticed in myself be protecting me?*

Validate the need for this protective response in the past. It can sometimes help to acknowledge the learned response and the preferred response.

I learned to push down my emotions in the past but now I am feeling my emotions. It is safe and normal to experience emotions.

These protective mechanisms are survival strategies. When someone's emotional needs weren't met in a safe or supportive way in the past, their brain and body adapt by finding ways to avoid or shut down feelings that could lead to emotional distress. While these mechanisms can offer short-term relief from painful emotions, over time they can limit emotional growth, lead to unhealthy coping patterns, and interfere with relationships or personal well-being.

Healing often involves learning to gradually allow emotions back in, creating a safer space for them to be felt, and challenging these protective responses when they no longer serve us. It may take time and support to unlearn the habits of emotional avoidance, but with practice, it's possible to build healthier emotional awareness and resilience.

Steps to Work With Your Protective Responses

How can I increase my tolerance and feel safer moving toward what I want? We can actively engage and work with protective responses to emotions by gradually building awareness, compassion, and new ways of relating to these reactions.

Awareness

The first step is recognizing the protective response. Notice when certain emotions trigger avoidance, tension, or reactive behaviors. Journaling, mindfulness practices, or tracking emotional patterns can bring these automatic responses into conscious awareness.

Name the Emotion and the Response

Once aware, it's important to name the emotion and the protective response. *I feel sadness right now, and my protective response is to shut down or distract myself.* By naming both, it helps to separate the emotion from the reaction and see them as distinct experiences.

Understanding the Purpose of the Protective Response

The protective response likely developed for a reason, often to shield against pain, rejection, or criticism. Acknowledging its original purpose with compassion can reduce feelings of shame or frustration. *This way of responding helped me feel safe as a child, but it's no longer needed in the same way.*

Explore the Underlying Beliefs

Protective responses are often tied to beliefs formed in childhood, such as *it's not safe to express anger* or *I don't deserve to feel joy*. We will discuss beliefs later. Just notice these for now.

Engage in Grounding Techniques

Protective responses were learned for a reason. They served a purpose. Here, we practice meeting them with curiosity, using the skills already explored to remain present with what arises.

Grounding techniques can support this process, helping you stay with the emotion rather than defaulting to automatic responses. If your breath has quickened, revisit the intentional breathing exercises practiced earlier. If sensations feel overwhelming, use gentle self-soothing strategies, such as patting your chest or feeling your feet against the ground. Chapters 6 and 7 further explore somatic strategies for each core emotion.

Practice Tolerating The Emotion

The next step is learning to tolerate the emotion without engaging in the protective response. This involves sitting with the discomfort and allowing the emotion to exist without rushing to fix or avoid it. Techniques like mindful observation riding the wave or self-soothing strategies can be helpful. We will dive deeper into strategies for each emotion later.

Riding the Wave of Emotion

Riding the wave of an emotion means allowing the feeling to rise, crest, and fall naturally without resisting or amplifying it. Like an ocean wave, emotions have a beginning, peak, and end. By staying present and noticing the sensations without judgment, you create space for the emotion to move through you.

Close your eyes or soften your gaze. Notice the emotion present, like a wave forming in the distance. Feel it rising within you, perhaps as warmth, tightness, or energy. Stay with it, breathing steadily, allowing the sensation to crest. Now, notice as it begins to shift, even slightly. With each exhale, imagine the wave gently rolling back, its intensity softening. Let it move through, knowing it will pass, like all waves do. When you're ready, bring your attention back to the present, feeling the ground beneath you, steady and constant.

Gradually, new responses can be cultivated. If fear leads to avoidance, practice small acts of courage to challenge that fear. If anger leads to suppression, practice expressing it assertively. These new responses should be small, manageable, and supportive of emotional growth.

If we are aware of what is happening now, accepting without judgment, we are better able to connect with the feelings, needs, and boundaries of our authentic selves. And make decisions and take action based on right now.

End-Of-Chapter Practice: Allowing The Emotion, Gently And Gradually

In this chapter, you have been exploring what it means to allow an emotion rather than manage it. Allowing is not about forcing yourself to feel more, or staying longer than is supportive. It is about giving an emotion enough space to exist so your body can do what it already knows how to do. This practice is an invitation to stay with an emotional experience in a way that honors both the feeling and your limits.

Begin by settling into your body. Notice where you feel supported. Feel the contact between your body and what is holding you. Let your breath move in its own rhythm.

Bring to mind an emotion that feels present and workable. Choose something that has a clear sensation in your body, but does not feel overwhelming.

Notice where you feel this emotion most clearly. Let your attention rest there. You are not trying to change the sensation or understand it. You are noticing that it is here.

As you stay with the sensation, notice how you are relating to it. You might find yourself bracing, holding, leaning away, or trying to contain it. Simply notice these responses. They are part of the experience, not a problem.

Now, see if you can allow the emotion in a way that feels supportive. You might stay with the center of the sensation, notice its edges, or hold it gently in your awareness without moving fully into it. Any of these is a form of allowing.

Remain with the sensation for a few breaths. Then, if it feels helpful, briefly widen your attention to a neutral or steady place in your body. Perhaps the feeling of your feet, your back against the chair, or your breath moving. After a moment, gently return your attention to the emotion. You can move back and forth like this, allowing pauses and returns. This is not leaving the emotion. It is supporting your capacity to stay.

As you continue, notice whether the sensation shifts in any way. It may soften, spread, intensify, move, or stay the same. You do not need to help it or guide it. Allowing includes letting the experience unfold in its own way.

You may notice thoughts about what the emotion means, where it came from, or what you should do about it. If so, acknowledge the thoughts and return your attention to the felt experience. Understanding is not required for allowing.

If it feels supportive, offer a simple phrase of permission, such as, *you are allowed to be here*, or, *I don't need you to go anywhere*, or, *I can stay with this for now.* Choose words that feel possible, not forced.

Notice whether your body begins to recognize this experience as intense but not dangerous. You are not trying to prove anything. You are noticing what your body learns through staying.

If at any point the experience moves outside your window of tolerance, gently shift your attention to your surroundings. Notice light, sound, or something you can touch. You can return to the sensation or end the practice as needed. Stopping is part of allowing.

Before closing, take a moment to notice what it was like to offer this kind of presence to your emotion. Not what changed, but what it felt like to stay in relationship with it, even briefly.

When you are ready, orient back to the room. Notice color, sound, and movement. Let your body settle, carrying with you the knowledge that you can allow an emotional experience without being overtaken by it.

Somatic Strategies for the Core Emotions

Objective: Learn somatic strategies for the core emotions.

You might not remember it but your nervous system does. – Victoria Erickson

Zen is not, in my view, philosophy or mysticism. It is simply a practice of readjustment of nervous activity. That is, it restores the distorted nervous system to its normal functioning. – Katsuki Sekida

The body whispers before it screams. Learning to listen is the beginning of regulation. – Irene Ortiz-Glass

Emotions don't just exist in the mind, they live in the body. Somatic awareness is the practice of noticing the signals the body sends and creating space to experience emotions without becoming overwhelmed by them. By building awareness of bodily sensations, we learn to work with our emotions rather than being swept away by them.

How do we stay with the felt experience of an emotion, fully allowing it, without becoming overwhelmed or shutting down?

The body speaks in sensation, and learning its language takes practice. What soothes one person may not work for another, and long-standing patterns don't shift overnight. But with repetition, the nervous system adapts, and what once required conscious effort gradually becomes second nature.

New responses often feel unnatural at first, requiring focused attention and active participation. Over time, your body will move toward regulation more instinctively, and you'll begin to recognize, sometimes only in hindsight, that your experience of emotion has changed.

These practices are designed to meet the body where it is at, helping you stay present while working with sensation rather than against it. Gently remember the 90 second wave and that emotions rise, peak, and shift when given space.

We are not erasing emotion but creating enough capacity to move through it. Each moment of connection with your body is a step toward ease.

Soothing The Body

What do the physical sensations I am having in my body need to allow and move through the emotion I am experiencing?

What do each of our emotions need for relief? In what ways can I move toward something that offers relief while continuing to allow my experience?

We will continue to stay with the felt experience. We are not solving the problem, fixing things externally, etc. We are calming the felt experience of the emotion in the body so we will be able to move into solutions with a clear mind and regulated body.

We may need to fill in gaps in learning for some emotions or all of the emotions.

You may have learned some of these strategies before and just need a refresher. Whatever the case, you are exactly where you need to be and doing a great job, in this present moment.

Quick Relief Techniques For Strong Emotions

These strategies can help reduce the intensity or flooding of the physical sensations of emotion to the nervous system. After, other strategies may be applied to continue to regulate the body.

Flood (verb)

Arrive in overwhelming amounts or quantities.

Shake

In the immortal words of Taylor Swift, "Baby, I'm just gonna shake, shake, shake, shake, shake. I shake it off, I shake it off." Stand up or stay seated, whatever is most comfortable for you, and shake your body. Shake your hands, wiggle, bend, reach up to the ceiling. Do the Hokey Pokey. Whatever feels good to your nervous system. Shoot for 15 seconds but 90 seconds is even better. A tambourine can really add to the magic here.

Sigh

This is the moment to use all your skills from high school theatre. Sigh with your whole body, channel your teenage self. Make the sigh audible. Sigh several times. Think of it as releasing the stored emotion from the body.

Ice Cube

Hold an ice cube in your hand or place it on your skin. The intense cold sensation can create a distraction and interrupt overwhelming emotions, helping to regain control and focus.

Cold Water

Splash cold water on your face or take a cold shower. This sudden change in temperature shocks the system, providing a momentary relief from intense emotions.

Breathe Cold Air

Inhale cold air deeply or spend time in a cold environment. Cold air inhalation triggers the body's relaxation response, reducing physiological arousal and promoting calmness.

Sour Candy

Consume sour candy or something really spicy. This serves as a grounding method, prompting you to concentrate on the present and interrupting the cycle of fear. This action signals to your brain that there's no imminent danger, helping to ease the intensity of your reaction and eventually bring it to a halt.

Vagus Nerve Exercises

In *Accessing the Healing Power of the Vagus*, Stanley Rosenberg describes simple practices designed to support the ventral vagal system, helping to encourage a shift out of fight or flight and toward a more regulated state. Below are two adapted versions.

The Basic Exercise

You can do this lying down, sitting, or standing. Gently interlace your fingers and place your hands behind your head for support. Keeping your head still, allow your eyes to slowly look to the right. Stay here and notice what happens in your body, waiting for a natural response such as a yawn, swallow, or sense of softening. When you are ready, bring your eyes back to center. Then repeat on the other side.

Rosenberg notes that eye position plays a role due to the connection between the muscles at the base of the skull and those that move the eyes.

The Half-salamander Exercise

Begin by keeping your head still and gently shifting your gaze to the right. From there, slowly tilt your head toward your right shoulder. Hold this position for about 30 to 60 seconds, noticing any shifts in your body. Return your head and eyes to center. Then repeat on the left side, again allowing time to notice any changes before returning to neutral.

Somatic Strategies For Each Core Emotion

While these exercises have been categorized by emotion, many if not all of them may be used for other emotions. This should be considered an exploration of what works best for you and your emotions.

Fear

Fear tightens the body, preparing it to flee or freeze. The chest constricts, breath shortens, and shoulders rise. In its subtler form, it's a quiet tension. At full intensity, it's a full-body jolt, a gripping pulse of adrenaline.

Fear and Hyperarousal

When fear pushes the body into hyperarousal, it becomes highly activated, ready to fight, flee, or react to a perceived threat. This state brings physical tension, racing thoughts, and a surge of energy. Fear can feel overwhelming here, creating a sense of urgency or panic. The body is primed for action, even if the threat is not clearly defined.

In hyperarousal, fear often shows up physically first. The heart may race, and the breath can become rapid and shallow. Muscles tend to tighten, especially in the chest, shoulders, and limbs, as the body prepares to move. Some people notice a fluttering or uneasy feeling in the stomach, or nausea caused by changes in blood flow. The senses may feel sharpened, with heightened sensitivity to sound, light, or movement. Thinking can become difficult as the mind jumps quickly from one thought to another, searching for solutions or escape. There may be restlessness, jitteriness, or a strong urge to act quickly or impulsively.

In this state, fear can feel too intense to contain. The body may react before there is time to reflect or assess what is actually needed. Often accompanied by sweating, trembling, and a tight or constricted feeling in the chest.

Fear and Hypoarousal

When fear moves into hypoarousal, the nervous system responds in a very different way. Instead of mobilizing for action, the body begins to shut down. This often happens when fear feels overwhelming and inescapable, and the nervous system shifts into a protective freeze or collapse response. Here, fear does not feel intense or urgent. Instead, it may feel distant, muted, or difficult to access at all.

In hypoarousal, fear is often experienced as numbness or emotional detachment. The body may feel heavy, sluggish, or difficult to move, as though weighed down. Heart rate can slow, and breathing may become shallow or irregular. There may be a sense of paralysis or an inability to take action, even when action is needed. Many people describe feeling foggy, disconnected, or far away from the present moment, with a strong urge to withdraw or hide both emotionally and physically.

In this state, the body is attempting to conserve energy and protect itself from emotional overwhelm. Rather than preparing for action, the body is prioritizing survival through withdrawal.

Framing Fear within the Window of Tolerance

The goal in both hyperarousal and hypoarousal is to return to a place where the fear can be felt and processed without overwhelming the body or shutting it down. In the window of tolerance, emotions like fear can be experienced without triggering survival responses.

In hyperarousal, the body needs to be soothed and calmed down so that the fear can be experienced without panic.

In hypoarousal, the body needs gentle reactivation, helping the person reconnect with the emotion and their body without being overwhelmed.

When fear is felt within this window, it can guide us toward taking protective action or making decisions that keep us safe, without leading to emotional dysregulation.

When my body is out of my window of tolerance, it is best for me to return to my window of tolerance before solving or fixing or thinking through this experience.

The body outside of its window of tolerance, especially in the emotion of fear, is not in problem-solving or fixing mode. It is in the land of emotions, often in the past, seeing through the lens of childhood emotional learnings or trauma. We must remind the body that the present is safe. We orient to the experience we are having in the present moment without framing it through what has happened before and what might happen in the future.

Right now, in this moment, I am safe.

Regulating Hyperarousal (Fight-or-Flight, Anxiety, Restlessness)

To bring the nervous system back into the window of tolerance from hyperarousal, the focus should be on gently calming and establishing a felt sense of safety in the present. The emotion of fear in hyperarousal needs excessive understanding. If someone was screaming in fear would you move into problem solving mode? Fear when experienced outside our window of tolerance needs to be grounded back into the present moment before taking action of any kind.

Weighted Comfort

Use a weighted blanket, heavy scarf, or firm hand pressure on your chest, shoulders, or thighs. Hold for at least 1-2 minutes while focusing on slow, steady breathing.

Self-rocking

While seated or standing, gently rock forward and backward or side to side in a slow, rhythmic motion. Imagine the movement calming your body like waves on the shore.

Cross-body Swiping

Using one hand, slowly stroke down the opposite arm, from shoulder to fingertips, applying light pressure. Repeat on both sides. Then swipe down the legs, from thighs to feet. This helps regulate overstimulation.

Humming or Vocal Toning

Take a deep breath in and exhale with a long hum or "voo" sound, feeling the vibration in your chest. Repeat 3–5 times. This engages the vagus nerve and calms the nervous system.

Forward-fold Resting

Sit at a table and rest your head and arms on the surface, or fold forward onto your lap if seated. Allow your body to feel supported and safe, breathing deeply into your belly.

Ground Pulse

Press your feet firmly into the ground for 3-5 seconds, then relax. Repeat several times, noticing the sensation of contact and stability with each press.

The Blue Dot

When I was young, my mother had terrible anxiety, the kind that keeps you from vacations, hockey games, and dancing with your friends. Every year, as we got in the car for our summer road trip, my grandmother would call out, "Last chance for happiness."

But she couldn't go. Her nervous system detected everything as a threat. That started to change when she was introduced to the blue dot.

Her therapist at the time, Clark Vinson, LCSW—Clark, if you're out there thank you for starting me on this path! — sent her home with a pack of blue dot stickers after their very first session. This was a session where he had offered to come to our house if she didn't feel she could make it to his office; it was long before telehealth. His understanding of why this might be hard gave her the confidence to try.

He told her to place the blue dots around the house and practice deep breathing whenever she noticed one. Soon, they were everywhere, on mirrors, in the car, on kitchen cabinets. To this day, I still instinctively take a deep breath when I see the *USA Today* logo because it was the exact same shade of blue.

This exercise is magnificent in its simplicity. It pairs an external cue with an internal response, creating a conditioned association between the blue dot and relaxation. It builds in a pause. It offers a natural, everyday way to practice regulation. And it trains awareness, shifting attention from distress back to something steady.

One little blue dot. Brilliant.

The Blue Dot Exercise

You can use any color or shape for this exercise, choose one that feels calming to you. It can be useful to pair this exercise with positive affirmations about safety and the present moment.

Place your sticker somewhere easily visible, like a wall, desk, or window.

Gently rest your gaze on the dot, letting your eyes settle without strain.

Inhale deeply through your nose, then exhale slowly through your mouth. Repeat for a few breaths.

I am safe here in this present moment.

I inhale safety and exhale fear.

Allow your body to relax in small ways, rolling your shoulders, loosening your jaw and the tension that settles in your face.

As you continue breathing, let your awareness expand beyond the dot. Notice colors, textures, sounds around you. If your mind wanders or distress increases, return your focus to the dot.

Continue for a couple of minutes, using both your breath and the dot to stay present.

Regulating Hypoarousal (Freeze, Collapse, Numbness, Disconnection)

To re-engage the body and mind and bring them back into the window of tolerance, the focus should be on gently reawakening the nervous system.

Somatic Tremoring

Stand with your knees slightly bent and allow your legs to gently tremble. You can also lie down and shake your arms and legs lightly. This helps release frozen fear and mobilize energy.

Expansion Stretching

Stand or sit upright and open your arms wide as if creating space around you. Inhale deeply as you stretch, then slowly exhale as you bring your hands to your chest. Repeat 3-5 times.

Pendulation Sway

While standing or seated, gently sway from side to side, shifting your weight slightly. Notice any sensation in your body as you move. This encourages nervous system flexibility.

Joint Compression

Apply gentle pressure to your knees, elbows, or shoulders by pressing them inward with your hands. Hold for a few seconds, then release. This increases body awareness and re-engagement.

Gentle Movement

Small, slow physical movements, such as stretching or walking, can help re-energize the body and reconnect with the present moment. Rocking your body, tapping, swaying, moving one limb, or a warm self hug can gently re-engage your body in the present moment. If full-body movement feels overwhelming, start small, wiggling fingers, shifting weight, or gently rolling shoulders can help reawaken sensation.

Sadness

Sadness weighs, it settles into the chest, the limbs, and the stomach. In small doses, it's a gentle heaviness. In full intensity, it can feel like sinking, gravity pulling inward.

Sadness and Hypoarousal

In hypoarousal, the body responds to sadness by shutting down or withdrawing. This state is often marked by numbness, disconnection, and a sense of heaviness, where the emotional weight of sadness can feel immobilizing. Rather than feeling sharp or intense, sadness may feel distant or muted, as if it is happening far away. Some people describe feeling flat, empty, or cut off from their emotional experience altogether.

Sadness in hypoarousal often shows up physically as heaviness in the limbs, sluggishness, or deep fatigue. The body may feel slow to move or resistant to action. There can be emotional numbness or detachment, making it difficult to cry or express sadness outwardly. Even though sadness is present, it may be hard to access fully. There is often a strong urge to withdraw, isolate, or shut down as the body conserves energy and protects itself from the weight of the emotion.

In this state, sadness can feel difficult to process, not because it is absent, but because the nervous system has moved into a protective, energy-conserving mode. The body may be attempting to shield itself from overwhelm, resulting in feelings of freeze, distance, or emotional quiet.

Sadness and Hyperarousal

When sadness moves into hyperarousal, it tends to show up with intensity and urgency. Instead of feeling muted, the sadness can feel overwhelming and consuming, often accompanied by agitation, anxiety, or panic. The emotional experience may feel unbearable, as though it cannot be contained or tolerated.

In hyperarousal, sadness is often expressed through intense crying or sobbing that feels difficult to control. The body may react with a racing heart, tightness in the chest, or shallow breathing. There can be restlessness or agitation, along with a sense of being emotionally flooded. Concentration often becomes difficult, as the intensity of the feeling takes over. Many people notice an urgent desire to escape the sadness, fix it quickly, or do something to make it stop.

In this state, sadness can feel like too much to handle at once. The body is highly activated, and the nervous system is working hard to manage the intensity of the emotion. The person may feel caught in a cycle of overwhelm, where the drive to escape or resolve the sadness comes from the body's attempt to find relief.

Sadness and the Window of tolerance

When sadness is experienced within the window of tolerance, it remains fluid and allows for connection, reflection, and meaning-making. Unlike the overwhelm of hyperarousal or the numbness of hypoarousal, sadness in this regulated state feels present but not consuming, a wave that moves rather than a weight that traps.

The body might feel heavier, with a natural tendency to slow down, but breathing remains steady, and there is still access to movement and self-expression. The throat might tighten briefly, but it does not feel completely blocked. Tears may come and go, but they do not feel like they will never stop.

Sadness in the window of tolerance allows for awareness and acceptance. There is an ability to reflect on why the sadness is there, to recognize its source, and even to find meaning in it. The sadness does not isolate, it may even deepen connection, leading to reaching out for comfort or sitting with the feeling in a way that fosters healing.

The body can express and release the emotion rather than suppressing it or becoming stuck in it.

This kind of sadness has a softness to it, it is tender rather than sharp, introspective rather than overwhelming, and it allows movement rather than freezing. It is sadness that flows, making space for eventual relief or even transformation.

Regulating Hypoarousal (Heavy, Numb, Disconnected, Shut-down Sadness)

When sadness leads to hypoarousal, it's helpful to think of it as a state of emotional "freezing" or withdrawal. The body is trying to avoid feeling the full depth of the sadness by shutting down or tuning out. Rather than pushing to "feel" the sadness more, the focus should be on gently re-awakening the body and mind through grounding, movement, and gentle reconnection with sensations. The goal is to slowly come back into your window of tolerance, where the sadness can be felt and processed.

These exercises aim to gently re-engage the body, increase awareness, and encourage movement to bring energy back into the system.

Heel Drops

Stand with your feet hip-width apart. Lift onto your toes, then let your heels drop down with a soft thud. Repeat slowly 5-10 times, noticing the vibrations moving through your legs.

Hand Rubbing and Brushing

Briskly rub your palms together to create warmth. Then, gently brush your hands down your arms and legs, noticing the sensation as you reconnect with your body.

Shoulder Rolls with Eye Shifts

Slowly roll your shoulders backward and forward in a circular motion. As you do, shift your eyes left and right, integrating movement and awareness.

Staccato Breathing

Inhale in three short sniffs through the nose, then exhale with one long sigh. Repeat 5 times to bring in a gentle sense of energy and presence.

Foot-tapping Sequence

While seated or standing, tap one foot quickly, then the other, alternating for 30 seconds. Pay attention to the rhythm and sensation as energy builds in your legs.

Reaching and Stretching

Stand or sit upright and slowly stretch your arms above your head, reaching as far as feels comfortable. Inhale deeply as you extend, feeling your chest and ribs expand. Hold for a few seconds, then exhale as you release your arms back down. Try stretching your arms out to the sides or in front of you, imagining reaching outward to connect with the world. Repeat 3-5 times, noticing any shifts in energy or sensation.

Regulating Hyperarousal (Agitated Sadness, Overwhelm, Restlessness, Crying That Feels Stuck)

When sadness leads to hyperarousal, the body is in a state of heightened alert, interpreting the emotion as something that needs to be resolved or escaped. Here, it's useful to think of the sadness as being "amplified" by the nervous system. Rather than diving into the sadness head-on, the focus should be on calming the body through grounding techniques, breathwork, or slowing down. The aim is to soothe the nervous system, bringing the intensity of the sadness back within the window of tolerance where it can be felt in a more manageable way.

Weighted Object on Abdomen

Lie down and place a small pillow, book, or weighted object on your stomach. Focus on the gentle pressure as you breathe deeply, feeling your belly rise and fall beneath the weight.

Wrist Soaking

Fill a bowl with warm water and submerge your hands or wrists. Notice the temperature and sensation, letting the warmth bring a sense of comfort and grounding.

Hand Tracing

Place one hand on a flat surface and, using the index finger of the other hand, slowly trace around each finger and the outer edge of your hand. Focus on the sensation of touch and movement.

Breath-led Swaying

While seated or standing, inhale deeply and gently sway forward slightly, exhale and sway back. Repeat in a slow, rhythmic motion, syncing your breath with the movement.

Visualization and Imagery

Visualization and imagery techniques are a powerful tool for calming the nervous system and promoting relaxation. By imagining yourself in a peaceful and safe environment, such as a serene beach or tranquil forest, you can evoke feelings of calmness and security. Visualizing specific details of the environment, such as the sound of waves or the warmth of the sun, can enhance the effectiveness of the practice. Guided imagery scripts or meditation recordings can provide additional support in guiding you through the visualization process.

Finding a Safe Haven (Adapted from the EMDR Calm Place Exercise)

Begin by finding a comfortable position, either sitting or lying down, whatever feels best to you. Close your eyes and take a deep breath in through your nose, filling your lungs completely. Slowly exhale through your mouth, letting all the tension melt away. Continue to breathe naturally and deeply for a few moments.

Now, I want you to imagine a place where you feel completely calm and at peace. This can be a real location you've visited, or a place entirely from your imagination. It can be a secluded forest, a serene beach, a cozy room, or even a fantasy world. Choose a place where nothing bad has ever happened and nothing bad ever will. This is your sanctuary.

As you settle into this safe haven, take a moment to look around. Notice the colors and images that surround you. What do you see? Are there trees, water, mountains, or something else? Is the sky blue, or is it a different color? Are there any other beings present: people, animals, or mythical creatures? Observe any weather patterns: is it sunny, breezy, or perhaps pleasantly cloudy? Whether you're indoors or outdoors, take in every detail.

Gently shift your focus to what you can feel. Notice the temperature in this place: Do you feel warm sunlight on your skin, or a cool, refreshing breeze? Are you wearing any specific clothing that adds to your comfort? Feel the textures around you, whether it's the softness of grass, the smoothness of stones, or the coziness of blankets. Sense any objects you might be holding or touching. Simply observe these physical sensations and how they contribute to your sense of safety and calm.

Turn your attention to the sounds within your safe haven. Do you hear the gentle rustling of leaves, the rhythmic waves of the ocean, or the melodious chirping of birds? Perhaps there is soothing music playing, or maybe it's perfectly silent. If there are people around, what are they saying? Listen carefully to any sounds or vibrations that add to the tranquility of this place.

Breathe in deeply and notice any fragrances that fill the air. Do you smell fresh flowers, the salty scent of the sea, or the earthy aroma of the forest? Maybe there's the comforting smell of your favorite food or a subtle fragrance that's hard to describe. Take in these scents and let them enhance your feeling of peace.

As you immerse yourself in this sanctuary, take a moment to appreciate how good and pleasant it feels to be here. Allow yourself to fully experience the calmness, safety, and happiness this place offers. Let all your senses, sight, touch, hearing, smell, and taste, enhance your feeling of well-being.

When you're ready, take a deep breath in through your nose and slowly exhale through your mouth. Begin to gently wiggle your fingers and toes, bringing awareness back to your body. Flutter your eyes open, feeling refreshed and peaceful. You can return to this safe haven anytime you need a moment of calm and safety.

∞∞∞

Whether sadness leads to hypoarousal or hyperarousal, the goal is to bring the nervous system back into a state where the emotion can be experienced without shutting down or becoming overwhelmed. This is the space where sadness can be felt, acknowledged, and moved through in a healthy way.

Anger

Anger burns in the body. Heat rises, muscles tense, and energy surges. In mild form, it's irritation. At its strongest, it demands movement, pushing, stomping, a need to discharge.

Anger and Hyperarousal

When anger moves into hyperarousal, the body becomes highly charged and ready for action. This state is marked by a surge of energy and an intense focus on defending or asserting oneself. Anger can feel explosive here, creating a strong sense of urgency to react, confront, or take control of the situation. The body is mobilized, alert, and prepared for conflict.

In hyperarousal, anger often announces itself physically. The heart may pound, and the breath can become rapid and shallow. Muscles tend to tighten, especially in the jaw, fists, shoulders, and arms, as the body prepares to fight or argue. Many people notice heat or flushing rising through the chest, neck, or face. There may be tightness in the chest or throat, as though the body is bracing for confrontation. Thoughts can race, often circling around a perceived wrong, boundary violation, or injustice. Alongside this activation, there is often a powerful urge to lash out verbally or physically, driven by the need to protect or assert oneself.

In this state, anger can feel overpowering and difficult to contain. Reactions may happen quickly, before there is time to pause or reflect. The sympathetic nervous system is highly activated, often accompanied by sweating, clenching, and a sense of being on edge, the body ready to explode.

Anger and Hypoarousal

When anger shifts into hypoarousal, the body responds in a very different way. When anger feels too overwhelming, unsafe to express, or unlikely to lead to change. Instead of moving outward, the anger turns inward or goes underground, leading to withdrawal or shutdown. The emotion does not disappear, but it becomes muted, buried, or difficult to access directly.

In hypoarousal, anger may be experienced as numbness or detachment from the feeling itself. The body can feel heavy, drained, or emotionally exhausted. Heart rate may slow, and breathing can become shallow. There may be difficulty thinking clearly, finding words, or expressing needs. Rather than feeling ready to confront, there is often a desire to withdraw, isolate, or avoid conflict altogether. Anger in this state may show up indirectly, through irritability, resentment, or passive-aggressive behavior.

In this state, the body is attempting to protect itself from the intensity of anger by conserving energy and reducing engagement.

Framing Anger Within the Window of Tolerance

Our aim in both hyperarousal and hypoarousal is to bring the body back to a place where anger can be felt and processed without overwhelming or shutting us down. Within the window of tolerance, anger can be experienced as a protective force, helping us assert boundaries and take action without losing control.

In **hyperarousal,** the body needs to be calmed so that anger can be expressed without destructive outbursts.

In **hypoarousal**, the body needs gentle activation to allow anger to be acknowledged rather than suppressed or ignored.

When anger is felt within the window of tolerance, it can guide us toward resolving conflicts or addressing injustices in ways that promote healthy boundaries and self-assertion.

Regulating Hyperarousal (Rage, Explosive Energy, Tension)

To bring the nervous system back into the window of tolerance, grounding techniques and calming exercises can be helpful. Anger in hyperarousal needs to be acknowledged without immediate reaction. If someone is raging in anger, we shouldn't rush to solve their problems right away. Instead, we ground ourselves and focus on the present moment before taking action. Techniques like deep breathing, muscle relaxation, and grounding exercises help diffuse the emotional charge, allowing anger to settle.

Hand Clenching and Release

Inhale deeply as you tighten your fists, feeling the tension gather. Hold briefly, then exhale as you slowly release your fists, imagining the anger dispersing with the movement. Repeat a few times, staying curious about the sensations.

Physical Expression with Awareness

Engage in movement that mirrors the energy of anger without suppressing or escalating it. Try pushing against a wall, squeezing a pillow, or stomping your feet while staying connected to your breath. Notice how the sensations shift as you engage with them.

Contained Sound Release

Find a private space and vocalize anger in a controlled way: humming, growling, or exhaling forcefully. This allows the activation in the body to release without overwhelming the system.

Temperature Shift

Anger often carries heat. Rinse your hands or face with cool water, hold an ice cube, or step outside if it's brisk. The contrast can help your nervous system register a shift while staying engaged with the emotion.

Symbolic Writing or Drawing

Without overanalyzing, let your hand move freely, scribbling, writing words, or drawing shapes that match the intensity of the feeling. Then, if it feels right, tear up or crumple the paper to externalize and release the energy.

Anger Release Practice

Begin by finding a comfortable seated position. This could be on the floor with crossed legs, on a cushion, or in a chair with your feet flat on the ground. The key is to sit in a way that allows you to be relaxed yet alert.

Take a moment to focus on your connection with the ground beneath you. Feel the weight of your body pressing down, and imagine roots extending from your body into the earth, anchoring you in place. This grounding technique can help create a sense of stability and security.

Begin to focus on your breath. Take slow, deep breaths, inhaling through your nose and exhaling through your mouth. Allow your breath to become steady and rhythmic, using it as an anchor to keep your mind present.

Acknowledge the presence of anger within you. Notice where you feel it most strongly. It might be a tightness in your chest, a clenching in your jaw, or tension in your shoulders. Bring your awareness to these physical sensations without judgment.

Imagine the anger as a tangible force within you, perhaps as a dark cloud or a ball of energy. Visualize this anger gathering in your hands, like you're scooping it up from within yourself.

With intention, slowly extend your arms out in front of you, palms facing away from your body. As you do so, imagine pushing the anger out of your body and into the space around you. You might visualize it dissipating into the air or being absorbed by the earth. Use vocalizations such as grunting or low screaming. Whatever feels best to you.

After pushing the anger out, slowly bring your hands back toward your body, allowing them to rest gently in your lap or at your sides. Take a few moments to notice any changes in how you feel. You may experience a sense of release, lightness, or calm.

If the anger persists or arises again later, you can repeat this process as many times as necessary to manage and diffuse it.

Regulating Hypoarousal (Shut Down, Suppressed Anger, Powerlessness)

When anger leads to shutdown, re-engaging the body and mind can help bring it back into balance. Movement, even subtle actions like stretching or shifting positions, helps reconnect the body with the emotion. Warmth, touch, and breath awareness can also ease the body back into a state of readiness to experience and process anger. Wrapping up in a comforting blanket or holding something warm helps restore a sense of safety, allowing the anger to surface and be acknowledged without being overwhelming.

Each of these strategies allows anger to be fully experienced and expressed while keeping the body engaged and present.

Strong Stance

Stand with your feet firmly planted, hip-width apart. Press your feet into the ground as if rooting yourself. Engage your leg muscles slightly and notice the connection to the floor. Hold for 30 seconds, adjusting your posture to feel more solid and steady.

Dynamic Arm Press

Place both hands against a solid surface (like a wall or table). Press firmly for 5-10 seconds, engaging your muscles. Release slowly and notice any changes in sensation. Repeat 3-5 times, allowing the strength to build gradually.

Jaw and Fist Engagement

Clench your jaw slightly, then release. Make a fist and squeeze for a few seconds, then slowly open your hand. Repeat both movements 3-5 times, noticing any shifts in sensation.

Grounded Marching

While seated or standing, lift one knee slightly, then the other, as if marching in place. Keep the movements slow but intentional. Focus on the sensation of your feet connecting with the ground. Continue for 30 seconds to 1 minute, noticing any increase in energy.

Postural Expansion

Stand or sit upright and slowly roll your shoulders back, opening your chest. Widen your stance slightly, pressing your feet into the ground. Imagine expanding outward, reclaiming space and strength in your body. Hold this posture for 30 seconds, noticing any shifts in sensation or energy. Repeat as needed, staying aware of the support beneath you.

Disgust

Disgust repels. It coils in the stomach, tightens the jaw, and pulls the body away. Subtle forms show up as aversion. At full intensity, it's a visceral need to expel.

Disgust and Hyperarousal

When disgust moves into hyperarousal, the body reacts quickly and forcefully. This response is often immediate and visceral, marked by a strong need to create distance from whatever feels offensive, unsafe, or contaminating. Disgust in this state is protective, mobilizing the body to reject or remove the source of discomfort.

In hyperarousal, disgust often shows up through sharp physical sensations. The heart may begin to race, and breathing can become shallow and quick. Many people notice a sudden wave of nausea or an urge to gag, as the body attempts to expel or block what feels intolerable. There may be tension around the stomach, throat, or face, along with a grimace or wrinkling of the nose, as the body tries to seal itself off. Thoughts can become focused on avoidance or escape, accompanied by an overwhelming urge to move away or eliminate the source of disgust as quickly as possible.

In this state, disgust feels intense and urgent. The nervous system is highly activated, driving a fight-or-flight response aimed at protection through rejection or removal.

Disgust and Hypoarousal

When disgust shifts into hypoarousal, the body's response becomes quieter and more withdrawn. This can happen when the experience of disgust feels overwhelming or impossible to process in the moment. Rather than pushing away forcefully, the body begins to shut down or turn inward as a form of protection.

In hypoarousal, disgust may be experienced as heaviness or emotional numbness, as if the feeling is too much to confront directly. Heart rate may slow, and breathing can become shallow. There may be difficulty expressing or even accessing the sensation of disgust, along with feelings of detachment from the offensive object or situation. Some people notice a dull, sinking feeling in the stomach or chest, paired with an urge to mentally or emotionally disconnect and retreat inward.

The body responds by reducing engagement and conserving energy, using shutdown and withdrawal to cope with the overwhelming sensation of disgust.

Regulating Hyperarousal (Gag Reflex, Nausea, Urgency to Push Away)

When disgust pushes into hyperarousal, focusing on deep breathing or grounding exercises can help slow the body's heightened reaction, allowing the disgust to be processed without becoming overwhelming. This helps to manage the intense physical reaction and regain control over the urge to escape or reject.

Grounding Through Neutrality

Disgust often creates a strong urge to reject or distance. Try anchoring in neutral physical sensations, like the pressure of your feet on the floor or the feeling of your breath in your nose, to prevent full-body recoil.

Breathing Into Softening

Disgust can tighten the throat, curl the body inward, or create a sense of expelling. A gentle breath into the tightness, especially focusing on an easy exhale, can help shift from immediate rejection to tolerating the experience.

Imagining Soothing Opposites

If disgust feels cold, rigid, or sharp, counterbalance it with imagery of warmth, fluidity, or softness. A warm drink, sunlight on the skin, or even the sensation of water washing over hands can shift the internal landscape without forcing change.

Palate Awareness

Press your tongue against the roof of your mouth for a few seconds, then release. Repeat a few times, noticing any shifts in sensation.

Hand to Mouth Connection

Lightly place a hand over your mouth without pressing. Breathe in through your nose and out through slightly parted lips. Notice any shift in the urge to gag or push away.

Sternum Circles

Using two fingers, rub small circles at the center of your chest. Apply gentle pressure and notice if it soothes nausea or tightness.

Regulating Hypoarousal

If disgust leads to shutdown, re-engaging with the body through light movement or sensory engagement can help bring the feeling back to the surface, allowing it to be acknowledged without emotional detachment. This can allow disgust to be felt without emotional numbness or avoidance.

Awareness Without Recoil

Notice how disgust shows up in your body. Instead of pulling away immediately, observe its qualities: Does your stomach clench? Does your skin crawl? Just naming the sensations can create space between the reaction and your response.

Slow Exposure to the Sensation

If disgust feels overwhelming, experiment with holding it just a little longer before shifting focus. This might mean imagining the source of disgust in a softer way or allowing your body to stay present without tensing against it.

Engaging the Tongue and Jaw

Yawn, hum, or stretch your tongue outward. This movement engages muscles that often tighten or go numb during hypoarousal. Engagement of tongue and jaw can reduce nausea and urge to gag.

Twisting Movements

Gently rotate your spine, turning side to side. Let the movement be fluid and natural, helping shift internal rigidity or aversion.

Alternating Arm Squeeze

Slowly squeeze one arm from the shoulder down to the hand, then switch sides. This rhythmic pressure can restore awareness to the body.

Upper Body Movement

Roll your head side to side or shake out your hands to reintroduce motion when disgust leads to withdrawal.

Surprise

Surprise startles. It jolts the breath, widens the eyes, and stiffens the body. In small doses, it's curiosity. When intense, it shocks the system into hyper-alertness.

Surprise and Hyperarousal

When surprise moves into hyperarousal, the body reacts instantly to the unexpected. This response is fast and reflexive, designed to orient toward sudden change. The nervous system mobilizes quickly, and the body becomes alert as it tries to assess whether what just happened is safe or threatening.

In hyperarousal, surprise often shows up as a sudden jolt in the body. The heart may jump or race, and the breath can catch or become shallow for a moment. Muscles may tense reflexively, especially in the shoulders, neck, or jaw. Many people notice their eyes widen, a rush of energy, or a quick intake of breath. Thoughts can feel scattered or blank at first, followed by rapid attempts to make sense of what just occurred. There is often a strong urge to orient, react, or move quickly in response to the unexpected.

In this state, surprise can feel sharp and activating. The sympathetic nervous system engages to support rapid assessment and action, even before conscious thought has caught up.

Surprise and Hypoarousal

When surprise shifts into hypoarousal, the body responds by slowing down or freezing. This can happen when the unexpected feels overwhelming, confusing, or too much to process all at once. Rather than mobilizing, the nervous system reduces engagement as a way to cope with the sudden change.

In hypoarousal, surprise may feel like a brief blankness or pause. The body can feel still, heavy, or momentarily disconnected, as if time has slowed or stopped. Breathing may become shallow, and there may be a sense of being frozen or unable to respond right away. Some people notice a foggy or distant feeling, along with difficulty organizing thoughts or actions. Instead of urgency, there may be a sense of withdrawal or delay before re-engaging with what is happening.

In this state, the body uses stillness and disengagement to protect against overload, allowing time to process the unexpected before moving forward.

Framing Surprise Within the Window of Tolerance

Surprise, in its various forms, can be experienced within the window of tolerance, allowing us to respond to the unexpected without becoming overwhelmed or detached. Whether it's a joyful surprise like seeing an old friend out of the blue or an unpleasant one like sudden bad weather, our nervous system can adjust if the surprise feels manageable.

Regulating Hyperarousal (Shock, Startle Response, Tension)

To balance surprise when it leads to hyperarousal, focus on slowing down the breath and bringing awareness to the present moment. This helps the body adjust to the initial shock or excitement without losing control. Grounding can help slow down the body's intense reaction, bringing focus back to the moment without rushing to act or react.

Gently acknowledge the surprise, allowing yourself time to process it.

Softening Startle Response

When the body startles, it often tenses up, holding onto the shock. To soften this response, start by closing your eyes briefly, then open them slowly with a long exhale. Lift your shoulders toward your ears, noticing any lingering tension, then let them drop with a sigh. Lightly brush your hands down your arms, releasing the startle from your body. Place both hands on your thighs, pressing gently to ground yourself as you take a slow breath. Repeat as needed, allowing your body to settle back into a sense of ease.

Blink and Release

Surprise can cause the eyes to widen and stay fixed. Intentionally blink slowly a few times, then squeeze your eyes shut for a second before re-opening. This helps reset the visual system and signals safety.

Finger Spreading and Closing

Extend your fingers wide, stretching them apart as much as possible, then slowly close them into a loose fist. Repeat a few times, noticing how the movement redirects activation.

Auditory Anchoring

Cup your hands over your ears for a few seconds, then release and listen carefully to the sounds around you. This shift in auditory input can help recalibrate the nervous system after a sudden jolt.

Diagonal Stretch

Stand tall and reach one arm across your body while extending the opposite leg slightly behind you. Hold for a moment, then switch sides. This cross-body movement supports reintegration after a shock response.

Awareness Without Immediate Reaction

Instead of jumping into action, pause and notice how the startle feels in your body. Is your chest tight? Are your shoulders lifted? Just naming these sensations can create space before reacting.

Grounding Through Physical Contact

Press your feet into the floor, place a hand over your heart, or hold onto something solid. This helps slow the nervous system's urge to stay in a heightened state.

Somatic smile

Find a comfortable position, laying down, seated or standing, whatever feels best to you. Relax your body with a few deep breaths. Close your eyes and focus on your breath, gently rolling your neck and loosening tension in your body.

Slowly create a gentle, soft smile on your lips. It can help to place the tip of your tongue on the roof of your mouth, just behind your front teeth. Imagine this smile spreading inward through your body, starting from your face and moving down to your chest and limbs. Maintain this gentle smile and focus on the feelings of warmth and relaxation it generates, letting these positive sensations permeate your body. Spend a few minutes in this state, and when ready, slowly open your eyes, noticing any shifts in your felt experience.

Regulating Hypoarousal (Freezing, Feeling Overwhelmed by Shock)

When surprise leads to a sense of detachment, try gently engaging the senses or moving the body to bring awareness back. Connecting with your surroundings, whether through sound, sight, or touch, can reawaken your capacity to fully feel the surprise.

Finger Tapping Sequence

Lightly tap each fingertip to your thumb in order, index, middle, ring, pinky, then reverse. Say the numbers 1-5 aloud as you tap, adding a cognitive anchor to bring attention back online.

Rhythmic Hand Drumming

Lightly drum your fingers or palms on your thighs, a table, or your chest in a steady beat. Repetitive rhythm helps stimulate engagement when energy feels low.

Ear Massage

Gently rub or tug your earlobes, then trace the outer edges of your ears with your fingers. The ears are connected to the vagus nerve, and this can encourage a return to alertness.

Knee Bounces

While seated, lightly bounce your knees up and down, keeping your feet planted. This subtle movement introduces energy back into the lower body.

Hand-to-Hand Squeeze

Press your palms together firmly, then release. Try interlacing your fingers and giving a gentle squeeze, focusing on the sensation of pressure and warmth between your hands.

Surprise has momentum. When regulated, it can transition into curiosity, alertness, or even excitement. When dysregulated, it can feel jolting or disorienting. These approaches help guide that momentum toward balance.

Surprise in Trauma

In the context of trauma, surprise often plays a critical role in how a traumatic event is experienced and remembered. Traumatic events typically involve an element of surprise, which can overwhelm the nervous system, leading to a fight, flight, or freeze response. This overwhelming surprise can contribute to the formation of intrusive memories, flashbacks, and other symptoms associated with post-traumatic stress disorder (PTSD). This imprinting is often amplified by the mismatch in emotional responses of others at the time of surprise. Due to this, normalization and validation of surprise as a normal experience to have is vital.

Tetris as a Tool for Negative Surprise

Studies have suggested that playing Tetris within hours of a traumatic experience can help reduce the occurrence of intrusive memories (flashbacks) associated with the trauma. The game's engaging and repetitive nature seems to compete with the process of memory consolidation in the brain, thereby lessening the impact of the trauma.

Healing happens in small, embodied shifts. Awareness builds not through grand gestures but through quiet moments, feeling the texture of fabric against the skin, noticing the rise and fall of breath, taking an extra second to savor warmth on the face.

Integrating somatic practices into daily life means catching moments of dysregulation *as they happen* and gently redirecting. A deep breath before a meeting, a grounding press of feet into the floor, a stretch to release tension, each act is a step toward increasing tolerance for emotional experience.

By tending to the body first, we expand our capacity to *feel* without fear.

To hold emotions as they are, without collapse or overwhelm. To stay present, connected, and engaged in the unfolding experience of life.

End Of Chapter Practice: Practicing A Somatic Response To An Emotion

In this chapter, you explored somatic ways of responding to emotions based on how they show up in your body. This practice is an opportunity to try one of those responses in real time. You are not trying to resolve an emotion or make it disappear. You are practicing listening to your body and offering it a supportive response.

Begin by settling into your body. Notice where you feel supported. Feel the contact beneath you. Let your breath move naturally.

Bring to mind an emotion that has been present recently. Choose something that feels manageable. Let the emotion come into awareness without amplifying it.

Notice how this emotion is showing up in your body right now. Where do you feel it most clearly? Let your attention rest there for a few breaths.

Next, notice your level of activation. Does your body feel charged, tense, or restless? Or does it feel heavy, slow, or distant? You might also feel somewhere in between. Let this noticing guide what comes next.

Now choose one somatic strategy from this chapter that fits how your body feels right now. There is no need to do more than one.

If your body feels activated, you might choose a strategy that offers grounding or containment. This could be feeling your feet, pressing your body gently into what supports you, lengthening your exhale, or bringing your hands to a steady place on your body.

If your body feels shut down or distant, you might choose a strategy that invites gentle engagement. This could be small movement, stretching, warmth, changing your posture, or orienting to something in the room.

If you feel relatively steady, you might choose a strategy that helps you stay connected, such as steady breathing, soft attention, or a supportive hand on your body.

As you use the strategy, stay with your body for several breaths. Notice what happens. Does anything shift, soften, or organize? Does the emotion feel more tolerable, even slightly? You are not looking for a particular result. You are noticing the response.

If nothing changes, that is information too. The practice is about learning what your body responds to, not about success.

Before closing, take a moment to acknowledge yourself. You might quietly say, *I am practicing*, or *I am learning how to respond to myself*, or *this makes sense in my body*.

When you are ready, gently orient back to the room. Notice light, sound, and color. Carry with you the felt sense of having offered your body a response rather than leaving it alone with the emotion.

Soothing strategies: Beyond the body

Objective: Learn soothing strategies beyond the body related to the core emotions.

Crying does not indicate that you are weak. Since birth, it has always been a sign that you are alive. – Charlotte Brontë, Jane Eyre

A mother holding her baby is one with her baby. If the mother is thinking of other things, the baby will not calm down. The mother has to put aside other things and just hold her baby. – Thich Nhat Hanh

How do we stay with the experience of an emotion, allowing it fully, while also finding ways to ease its intensity?

Soothing extends beyond the body. While somatic strategies form the foundation, relief can also come through imagery, external comfort, sensory engagement, or meaningful connection with others. Some find grounding in physical sensations helpful, while others need cognitive, relational, or environmental support. No single approach fits every person or every moment. Experimentation is key.

Change happens through practice. At first, shifting emotional responses requires effort, awareness, intention, and patience. Over time, your system will integrate what works, and you'll begin to respond with greater ease.

This chapter expands on ways to care for emotions beyond direct somatic engagement. These strategies are meant to help you regulate while maintaining presence. Gently remember the 90 seconds and that emotions rise, peak, and shift when given space.

The goal is not to control emotion but to support yourself through it. Every small act of care strengthens your ability to stay present. Wherever you are in this process, you are exactly where you need to be.

Reparenting The Emerging Self

Imagine your newly formed self as a curious, boundary-testing toddler, gloriously 3 years old, eager to explore. What would they need to navigate big emotions? How would you support this younger version of yourself in feeling, expressing, and releasing each core emotion?

Using gentle parenting as a guide, consider how you would respond to a child moving through enjoyment, sadness, anger, disgust, fear, or surprise. The following examples illustrate ways caregivers support children in processing emotions, offering a blueprint for how you might nurture your own emotional experience with the same patience and care. You can use these gentle responses to be a good caregiver to yourself.

Fear

Acknowledge the child's fear and reassure them that it's okay to feel scared sometimes.

Provide comfort by explaining that they are safe and you are there to protect them.

Encourage the child to take small, manageable actions that can help them feel more in control of their fears, such as holding a flashlight in the dark or practicing deep breathing to calm their body.

Sadness

Acknowledge the child's sadness and let them know it's okay to feel this way.

Offer hugs, kind words, and a listening ear to provide comfort and support.

Encourage the child to express their sadness through creative outlets such as writing, drawing, or playing music.

Anger

Teach the child techniques such as deep breathing, counting to ten, or taking a break to help them regulate the sensations in their body when feeling angry.

Encourage the child to express their anger in healthy ways, such as talking about it or expressing it creatively.

Encourage the child to participate in an active game or sport that they enjoy, such as playing catch, kicking a soccer ball, or jumping on a trampoline. Physical activity can help reduce stress and promote a sense of well-being by releasing endorphins, the body's natural mood elevators.

Disgust

Validate the child's feelings of disgust and let them know it's okay to feel this way.

Help the child find alternatives or solutions when faced with something they find disgusting.

Allow child choices related to disgust.

Provide gentle encouragement to explore new things.

Surprise

Explain that feeling surprised is a natural reaction to unexpected events or situations.

Encourage the child to explore their feelings of surprise and talk about what surprised them.

Emphasize the excitement and wonder that can come with surprises, turning them into positive experiences.

Enjoyment

Encourage the child to share their joy with others, whether through talking about it, drawing a picture, or expressing it in another creative way.

Join in the child's joy by celebrating their achievements or happy moments together, reinforcing the positive emotions they're experiencing.

Prompt the child to reflect on what they're grateful for, fostering a sense of appreciation and happiness.

Strategies For The Core Emotions

You will notice almost all of these strategies can be adjusted for any of the core emotions. Consider these ideas a place to start in your journey to discover what you need. Explore how the physical sensations and emotions respond. You may notice more than one emotion and need several strategies. Regardless, you are right where you are supposed to be here in the present moment.

Here, we'll remember that life will have sad and scary and disgusting and surprising and angering and the happiest of moments. That is the way of life and being human. Our goal is to experience the emotions of life while remaining in our window of tolerance.

Fear

Fear is an unpleasant emotional state that arises when something is perceived as threatening or likely to cause harm. It is a rapid, body-based response shaped by both present experience and past learning, organizing the body for protection through escape, avoidance, or stillness.

Fear keeps us focused on the past or worried about the future. If we can acknowledge our fear, we can realize that right now we are okay. Right now, today, we are still alive, and our bodies are working marvelously. Our eyes can still see the beautiful sky. Our ears can still hear the voices of our loved ones. – Thich Nhat Hanh, Fear: Essential Wisdom for Getting Through the Storm

Fear speaks through sensation. It arrives quickly, often before thought. A sudden tightness in the chest, a held breath and a pulse that jumps. The body alerts us long before the mind catches up.

Imagine standing at the top of a dark set of cellar stairs, the air cool and still, the smell of damp earth rising from below. Even the image may shift something inside you. A flutter in the stomach, a shiver along the back, and a spike in alertness. Fear often begins this way, as a physical signal that something feels unknown or unsafe.

Fear is a protective emotion that asks, *am I safe?* Fear does not need to be fought or silenced. It needs acknowledgement.

I am experiencing fear.

I am scared.

It is normal to experience fear.

Everyone feels afraid sometimes.

Responding to fear in this gentle way may feel strange at first. Perhaps you learned to push it down or ignore it. Perhaps you join fear's story immediately, climbing into thoughts that amplify the sensation. Or maybe you learned to go to war with your fear, trying to outthink or outpace it.

But fear, like all emotions, wants to be felt and moved through. The following practices help soothe the nervous system so fear does not have to take over your inner world.

Establish And Affirm Safety

Safety

The condition of being protected from harm and danger.

I am able to assess danger and take action to keep myself safe as needed.

I am able and willing to provide safety to myself.

Emotional safety is the state of feeling secure, supported, and accepted in expressing one's thoughts, feelings, and vulnerabilities without fear of judgment, criticism, or reprisal. In emotionally safe environments we feel comfortable being ourselves, can share our emotions, and engage in open and honest communication.

Safety With Self

Pause for a moment and ask yourself if you are emotionally safe with yourself. Notice how it feels to consider that question. How does your body respond? Does your stomach clench or your breath shorten? Do you feel a wave of unease or perhaps a lightness? Maybe you scoff or laugh.

Whatever arises, just notice, it is simply information.

Emotional safety with self means being someone you can turn toward rather than someone you fear. It means you can bring your sadness, fear, anger, or disappointment to yourself without being met with punishment, dismissal, or abandonment.

For many people, internal safety feels unfamiliar because the early handoff of care was never fully completed. In childhood, caregivers regulate us through consistency, presence, and attunement. Their bodies set the rhythm that helps our nervous system learn what safety feels like. Over time, this care is meant to move inward so that we learn how to soothe, protect, and respond to ourselves.

But if a caregiver was afraid, overwhelmed, unpredictable, or unavailable, that transfer may not have occurred. You may have learned that your needs were too much, or that you had to stay small to stay safe. You may have learned to scan for danger instead of comfort. Self-care may now feel foreign, indulgent, or unsafe because at one time it was.

This is an adaptation. Your nervous system shaped itself around what was required to survive your early environment.

Safety in self grows through small, steady acts of care. Eating on a regular schedule. Sleeping enough. Moving your body. Checking in with your emotions rather than bracing against them. Seeking comfort instead of numbing. Each act says to your nervous system, *I will not ignore my own needs. I will not abandon myself.*

Ask yourself, *am I caring for myself the way a good caregiver would?* Notice what comes up. Self-care is not a luxury. It is the foundation on which internal safety is built. Without tending to these basics, it is difficult for the body to trust you.

It may feel uncomfortable to place yourself at the center of your own care. Many people fear they will become selfish, unrecognizable, or unlovable if they stop prioritizing everyone else. The mind whispers, *what will they think of me?* But most people are not thinking of you nearly as intensely as you fear. Caring for yourself does not take anything away from others. It restores your capacity to be present.

Resistance is normal. You may feel guilt, avoidance, numbness, or a strong pull to distract yourself. These reactions were once protective. Turning inward might have been dangerous, overwhelming, or met with criticism. The body remembers that. Offer compassion for the parts of you that learned self-protection instead of self-connection.

Safety in self begins with neutrality. You lay down the internal weapons you once needed. You stop fighting your own needs. You create a space inside where you can meet yourself with steadiness instead of fear. You remind yourself that you are worthy of care not because you have earned it, but because you exist.

Ask yourself gently, *what would I be doing if I felt safe with myself? What would I stop doing? How does safety feel in my body? What is one small step I can take today that moves me closer to that feeling?*

Internal safety is learned over time. It grows with each moment you choose kindness over criticism, presence over avoidance, and care over abandonment. Little by little, you become the caregiver you need and needed.

Reclaiming Developmental Milestones Through the Body

Sometimes, the gaps in our ability to self-soothe, trust, or connect aren't just patterns, they're missing developmental building blocks. Erik Erikson, a developmental psychologist, described a series of psychosocial stages that shape how we relate to ourselves and the world. When these stages are interrupted, skipped, or distorted by trauma or inconsistency, the work of adulthood often becomes learning what wasn't offered to us when we needed it most.

The good news is that the body remains capable of learning at any age. We do not need to recreate childhood, but we can offer ourselves the kinds of experiences the nervous system missed. The following practices draw from early developmental tasks and translate them into simple invitations of rebuilding.

Trust vs. Mistrust (Infancy)

Core task: Learning that the world is safe and needs will be met.

Adult Practice

Wrap yourself in a blanket or apply gentle pressure (weighted blanket or hand to chest). Say aloud: *My needs matter. I can meet them with kindness.*

Pair this with consistent routines: waking, sleeping, eating. Try a "soft landing" ritual at the end of your day: warm tea, soft light, hands on heart and belly.

Show up for your basic self care needs. It is next to impossible to establish self trust if you are not feeding, watering, playing and adequately resting self.

Autonomy vs. Shame and Doubt (Toddlerhood)

Core task: Developing independence and confidence.

Adult Practice

Choose a small decision to make entirely for yourself: what to eat, what to wear, where to walk. Say: *I trust my choices.*

Use movement (marching, strong stance) to embody autonomy.

Practice saying *no* to something small, without explaining.

Walk barefoot for a few steps and say: *I know where I stand.*

Initiative vs. Guilt (Preschool Age)

Core task: Initiating action, asking questions, exploring.

Adult Practice

Try a creative act with no outcome goal, doodle, sing, move freely. Allow curiosity without productivity. Say: *It's safe to try. I don't have to be perfect.*

Revisit something playful from your childhood: jumping jacks, hop-scotch, sidewalk chalk, exploration.

Ask yourself: *What do I want to try just for fun?*

Industry vs. Inferiority (School Age)

Core task: Building skill and experiencing accomplishment.

Adult Practice

Do something slightly challenging (such as learning a recipe, organizing a space, etc.). As you work, say: *I am capable. I can learn as I go.*

Notice your posture. Can you sit or stand with pride?

Set a tiny goal and celebrate completing it without comparing to others.

Identity vs. Role Confusion (Adolescence)

Core task: Exploring and owning your authentic self.

Adult Practice

Journal for 5 minutes: *What feels most like "me" right now?* or *what am I drawn to and why?* Then sit in stillness, feeling into your body's response. Say: *I belong to myself.*

Ask yourself: *What do I value most right now? What feels like me?*

Wear something expressive or play music that feels personal.

Make a "Me" board, digital or paper, images, colors, quotes that feel like you today.

Journal: *What am I not pretending about anymore?*

Safety With Others

How do you know when you are safe with someone? Do you feel a sense of ease, warmth, or steadiness? Or does your body tighten, your breath shorten, your thoughts scanning for possible harm? Safety, or the lack of it, shows up in the body before the mind makes sense of it.

Safety with others begins in early relationships. Caregivers model what it means to be safe or unsafe in connection. Some teach that others are reliable, attuned, and responsive. Others teach that connection comes with inconsistency, harm, or obligation. Over time, these experiences shape how we navigate closeness, distance, and trust.

Fear in relationships often stems from past breaches of safety: betrayals, neglect, violations of boundaries. We may find ourselves hypervigilant, expecting harm, or avoiding connection altogether. Safety is not about removing fear but learning when it is a relic of the past and when it is a true signal.

What would I be doing if I felt safe with others? What would they be doing? How does safety feel in my body? What small steps can I take to move toward it?

We do not have to force connection or override our protective instincts. Instead, we listen. We notice which relationships invite us to soften, which require us to brace, and which spaces feel safe enough to exhale.

Co-Regulation

Co-regulate

Soothe or move through the felt sensations of emotion with the support of a close other. These are supportive, consistent responses to reduce emotional arousal and increase feelings of safety.

When our nervous system is experiencing the physical sensations of fear, finding safety in others can be tricky business. Our experience of the external and internal world are heightened, we may be in fight or flight and unconsciously detecting safety and danger cues from others and the environment.

The safest person may not feel safe.

We will remember our newly formed self here, our caregivers and how they might respond to strong emotions. A lowered tone, soothing noises, gentle pats on the back or maybe a hug.

We will remember that the idea is to ask for help with or share the emotion we are experiencing. We are asking for help regulating back to baseline, we are not looking to the close other to solve our emotional experience. Or join us in thinking the sensations and emotions we are experiencing. It is easy to slip into externalizing our inner dialogue when seeking co-regulation with others. Like most things, there is a balance. Move toward regulation of the felt sensations first.

Things to consider when seeking to co-regulate. *How does a person who feels safe to you during feelings of fear respond? How would your nervous system feel? Do they offer advice, hug you, make soothing noises? Which do you prefer?*

Sometimes your partner is the safe person for co-regulation, and sometimes it's a friend or a family member. Consider your audience. If you have just had a screaming fight with your partner, their own emotions may make them unable to co-regulate.

Asking for Co-regulation

Take a moment to notice what your body is feeling. Before reaching out, ask yourself: *What kind of support would feel most regulating? Do you need presence, a hug, soothing words, or just someone to sit beside you?*

When you're ready, approach your chosen person and express your need clearly. Try saying, *I'm feeling overwhelmed, can you sit with me for a moment?* or *I need some reassurance. Can you remind me that I'm safe?* If words feel difficult, nonverbal requests, such as holding out a hand or leaning in for contact, can also communicate your need for connection.

As you receive support, focus on how your body responds. Does your breath slow? Do your shoulders drop? If something doesn't feel helpful, gently adjust. *Could we just sit quietly?* or *can you hold my hand instead?* This process strengthens your ability to recognize and seek the co-regulation that best supports you.

Perhaps you are uncertain of your co-regulation needs, the following components of co-regulation are a good place to start exploring.

Components of Co-regulation

Active Listening: Listen attentively to the other person without judgment or interruption. Validate their feelings by acknowledging their emotions and experiences. Co-regulation is not the time to jump on the bandwagon with or amplify the other's experience.

A note on listening: When co-regulating, it helps to think of what the person in distress might need. That often means space for what they are experiencing. Sometimes we relate to others by sharing a similar story of our own (this is neither good or bad, right or wrong, only a style of relating), however a distressed person desiring co-regulation generally needs the moment to be about them in order to feel heard. It is ok to ask "do you want me to listen or give advice or distract you?" if you feel unclear what will help.

Empathy and Validation: Show empathy by putting yourself in the other person's shoes and acknowledging their feelings as valid. For example, you might say, "I understand why you feel that way."

Offer Comfort and Reassurance: Provide comfort and reassurance by offering physical gestures like a hug, holding hands, patting their back or sitting close. Offer words of encouragement and support. Use fewer words.

Stay Calm and Present: Maintain a calm and composed demeanor, even if the other person is upset or agitated. Your calm presence can help them feel more secure and regulated. Be a warm and calming presence. Keep a gentle tone and a soft voice. Move slowly.

Model Self Regulation Techniques: When co-regulating with someone who is in a heightened state of distress, your own nervous system may become activated. It can be helpful to yourself and the person in distress to model self regulation techniques. This can be as simple as doing a soothing strategy yourself. Slow your own breathing, people often match breathing rates. Dim the lights. Reduce the noise level. Reduce visual stimuli. Take a few deep breaths or shake out your own body. Ask for a brief pause.

Reflective Responding: Reflect back what the other person is saying to ensure you understand their perspective. This can help them feel heard and validated. Labeling the emotion can be helpful here. Be prepared to get it wrong.

Problem-solving Together: If appropriate (the person seeking to co-regulate has specifically asked), work together to find solutions to the problem or stressor. Collaborate on finding constructive ways to address the issue.

In the case of circumstances that require a solution, set aside time to problem solve later.

Provide Distraction or Diversion: Sometimes, offering a distraction or engaging in an enjoyable activity together can help regulate emotions. This could be watching a movie, going for a walk, or doing a favorite hobby.

Set Boundaries: While providing support, it's essential to maintain your own boundaries and well-being. Be clear about what you can and cannot offer in terms of support, and encourage the other person to seek additional help if needed.

Predictable Routines — Anchoring in Familiarity

When emotions feel overwhelming, predictable routines provide a sense of structure and safety. Engaging in familiar habits reminds the nervous system that there are stable, reliable elements in daily life.

Choose a simple routine that brings comfort, a morning coffee ritual, an evening walk, or a favorite playlist at the start of the day. Engage in it with full awareness, noticing the small, repetitive actions. If the body feels unsettled, remind yourself, *I have done this before, and I will do it again,* allowing the rhythm of the routine to provide steadiness.

Comforting Narratives

Fear can make the world feel unpredictable, but familiar stories, music, or environments provide a sense of stability. Returning to a favorite book, movie, or song can remind the nervous system that not everything is uncertain.

Choose a story, song, or movie that has brought comfort in the past. Let yourself engage fully, reading aloud, singing along, or watching with the intention of absorbing its familiar rhythm. If fear feels overwhelming, pair this with a cozy physical environment, like a warm blanket or a dimly lit space.

Sadness

Sadness is an emotional state of unhappiness, ranging in intensity from mild to extreme and usually aroused by the loss of something or someone highly valued or an unmet longing.

The word 'happy' would lose its meaning if it were not balanced by sadness. – Carl Jung

Sadness often enters as a slowing in the body, a heaviness in the chest, a tug behind the eyes, and a hollow ache in the stomach. It is the emotional imprint of loss and longing.

Imagine a cherished friend moving away or the quiet end of a relationship. Notice how your body responds. Your shoulders slump. Your breath becomes shallow. Your throat tightens. These signals are the body's way of saying something has shifted.

Begin by acknowledging the emotion without judgment. Humans are meant to feel sadness. It reflects connection and meaning.

I am experiencing sadness.

I am sad.

It is normal to feel sadness.

Everyone feels sad sometimes.

Sadness does not need to be solved or rushed. It needs room, breath, and presence. The following practices help sadness move through the body in a way that feels gentle and supportive.

Crying

A note on crying: It is okay to cry. Crying is cleansing and helps us process through felt sensations and emotions. We cry during sadness and fear and happiness and anger and joy and excitement and surprise.

Crying helps release sadness by engaging both physiological and emotional processes that facilitate movement through the feeling rather than staying stuck in it.

Tears contain stress hormones and natural painkillers, which can reduce tension and create a feeling of relief. The activation of the parasympathetic nervous system during and after crying promotes a shift from distress to regulation. Breathing patterns change, often deepening after a cry, helping to settle the body.

Emotionally, crying serves as an expression of sadness that allows it to be processed rather than suppressed. The physical sensations, tears, trembling breath, the loosening of the throat, help externalize internal emotions, making them feel less trapped. The body's tension shifts, often leading to lightness or openness afterward.

Crying introduces movement, waves of feeling, breath, and sensation, which can prevent stagnation and allow a return to connection. When met with self-compassion or co-regulation, crying can also signal safety, reinforcing that it's okay to feel and move through emotions.

Connecting with Crying: A Guided Practice

Find a quiet, comfortable place where you won't be interrupted. You may want a blanket, tissues, or a comforting object nearby. Take a moment to acknowledge why you are here. Not to force tears, but to allow yourself space to feel. Place both feet on the ground or settle into a supported position.

Do you feel resistance to crying? It might show up as a lump in your throat, a tightness in your chest, or a holding in your jaw. You don't need to force anything, just notice what's there. Where does the resistance sit in your body? How does it feel?

Rather than pushing it away, see if you can sit with it. Breathe into it. You are safe.

You may notice a sensation in your nose, like the flutter of an unformed sneeze. Or a pressure behind your eyes, the weight of something unspoken. Maybe your throat tightens, the lump still lingering, caught between holding back and letting go.

Let yourself observe these sensations without changing them. Just be with them.

Take a slow, steady breath. As you exhale, let your shoulders drop just a little. Feel the ground beneath you, solid and unwavering. It can hold you.

You are allowed to let go.

Place your right palm on the left side of your chest. Tap gently, rhythmically. Notice the steady thud beneath your hand, the quiet reminder that you are here.

Crying is a natural response to emotion. It does not need to be explained or justified.

Breathe deeply, filling the space around the lump in your throat. Imagine warmth spreading through it, softening its edges, loosening its grip.

If tears begin to form, allow them. Maybe they come as a single drop, a slow release. Maybe they stay just beneath the surface, waiting. However they arrive, trust the process.

If there is hesitation, breathe again. Let yourself sink into the support beneath you. Notice the way your body responds.

Perhaps the lump changes, becoming lighter, shifting, dissolving. Maybe it moves through you, finding its own way out. There is no right way to release, no perfect way to cry.

I am safe.

I am allowed to feel.

I am allowed to cry.

Stay as long as you need. When you're ready, place a hand over your heart and take one final deep breath. Notice how your body feels now. Let yourself return gently, carrying the permission to release whenever you need.

If tears came, notice how your body feels now. If they did not, that is okay too. Connection takes time. Place a hand over your heart. Say, internally or aloud: *I honor my emotions. I allow myself to feel. I am safe.* Wiggle your fingers, notice the room around you, and gently transition back into your day.

Slow Down

Sadness is an invitation to slow down and treat yourself with tenderness. It invites self-compassion, reminding you to take care of your emotional and physical needs during challenging times.

Take care of these needs by getting enough sleep, eating right, and moving your body.

While it's important to allow yourself to feel sad, it's also important to engage in activities that bring you enjoyment and fulfillment. This could be anything from exercise to creative pursuits to spending time with loved ones.

Eat the ice cream, order the pizza, stay in your pajamas for a day or two. Swaddle yourself in your favorite blanket and watch your favorite comfort show.

Creative Expression: Giving Form to Sadness

Sadness can feel heavy when it stays inside with no outlet. Creative expression offers a way for the emotion to move. It gives sadness a shape outside the body so it no longer has to be carried alone.

Begin by noticing where sadness sits in your body. Maybe it feels thick in your throat, heavy in your chest, or weighted in your limbs. Let the location of the emotion guide you toward the kind of expression that might help it move.

If sadness feels tight in your chest or throat, writing may help. Sit with a pen and paper and let your hand move. You can write a sentence, a list of words, or even scribble shapes that match the feeling. You do not need to explain anything. You are letting the sadness speak in whatever form comes naturally.

If sadness feels muted or wordless, visual art can be a place to hold it. Choose a color that reflects the emotion and press it onto paper. Make shapes that match the heaviness or the ache. This can give the emotion a place to rest.

If sadness feels like a slow ache in the ribs, music may be the language it understands. Play a song that matches your mood. Let yourself hum or sing if it helps. Notice how the vibration of your voice shifts the feeling inside.

If sadness feels heavy in your limbs, movement may help it travel. Stretch slowly, sway your body, or take a short walk. Move as gently as the emotion requires. There is no choreography. You are letting sadness flow through you instead of staying trapped.

Creative expression is not about fixing sadness or turning it into art, you are offering the emotion a doorway. Once sadness is expressed, even in the smallest way, the body often feels a little more spacious, a little less burdened, and a little more able to breathe.

Connect with Nature

Nature has a natural regulating effect, offering a shift in perspective and a reminder of the larger world beyond internal emotions.

Step outside or bring your focus to an element of nature nearby, whether it's a plant, a breeze through an open window, or the sound of birds. Notice the details: the textures, colors, or patterns. If possible, physically engage by touching the bark of a tree, feeling the grass, or dipping fingers into water. Let the body take in the sensory cues, allowing nature's steadiness to influence your internal state.

It is also always okay to set your sadness aside and experience the present moment fully when desired or needed. Use the container exercise to practice gently setting aside.

Anger

Anger is an emotional state that arises when something feels interfering, unjust, or harmful. It emerges when a boundary has been crossed, a value violated, or an action feels wrong. Anger is a protective signal from the body, alerting us that something is significant and that a response may be needed. Anger mobilizes energy. It prepares the nervous system for action, not necessarily aggression, but movement, protection, or change. Rather than telling us what is wrong with us, anger tells us what is not acceptable or sustainable.

Anger is just anger. It isn't good. It isn't bad. It just is. What you do with it is what matters. It's like anything else. You can use it to build or to destroy. You just have to make the choice. –Jim Butcher, White Night

Anger shows up quickly in the body. It rises as heat in the chest, a rush of energy in the limbs, and a tightening in the jaw. It is the body's way of saying something feels unfair or out of alignment. Anger is not a sign of danger. It is a signal that a boundary has been crossed or a need has gone unmet.

Imagine standing in a crowded coffee shop when someone suddenly cuts in front of you. Feel the quick spark of heat, the sharpness in your breath, the way your muscles tense, preparing to act. Anger often begins in this way, through sensation rather than thought. Your body reacts before your mind has even begun to name the experience. This is anger asking for attention.

Anger is a protective emotion, yet many of us learned to fear it, silence it, or express it only through action. You may have been taught that anger is unsafe, unacceptable, or something to hide. Or you may feel compelled to act immediately the moment anger appears, trying to discharge the intensity before you ever feel it.

But anger does not need to be eliminated or rushed. It needs space, breath, and presence. Before you try to reason with it, solve it, or translate it into words, anger needs to be acknowledged with gentleness.

I am experiencing anger.

I am angry.

It is normal to feel anger.

Everyone feels angry sometimes.

Anger shows me something is important to me.

Anger is allowed here.

Anger asks for space before action. Before we try to understand it or do anything with it, we begin by meeting the physical sensations it brings. These practices help your body find steadiness so the emotion can move through without overwhelming you.

Pause

When we notice the emotion of anger rising within us, pausing offers a powerful opportunity to respond thoughtfully rather than react impulsively. Anger, by its nature, urges us toward immediate action, often demanding a quick release of its energy. However, taking a moment to pause can create space between the emotion and our reaction, allowing us to choose a response aligned with our values rather than driven by the intensity of the moment.

Pausing when anger emerges gives us a chance to tune into our physical sensations, notice the racing heart, tightened muscles, or the heat rising in the body. This awareness shifts us from autopilot to mindful observation, helping us to engage with the emotion without being overwhelmed by it. In this space, we can ask ourselves: what is the anger signaling, is there a boundary that needs to be set, or perhaps a need that isn't being met? Just notice. We will address these later.

This pause is not about suppressing anger but about allowing it to be felt and understood without rushing into action. It's a moment of self-regulation, where we ground ourselves and reconnect with a sense of choice. Techniques like taking a deep breath or physically stepping away from the situation can further deepen this moment of reflection.

By pausing, we reclaim the power to respond consciously, transforming anger from a force that controls us into a tool for clarity, self-assertion, and healthy communication.

Pause and Notice

Take a moment to pause. Close your eyes or soften your gaze. Feel the weight of your body against the chair or the floor beneath your feet. Notice the texture of the air as it moves in and out of your nose.

As you pause, become aware of your surroundings. What do you hear? The hum of distant sounds, the quiet rustle of fabric? Let each sound come and go without attaching to it.

Feel the stillness within the pause, allowing yourself to be fully present in this small moment, without needing to change anything. Simply notice what is.

Scream Into the Void

Quiet scream or scream out loud if it won't disturb the neighbors and sometimes even if it will.

A quiet scream practice is a way to release anger in a controlled manner without using your voice but still engaging the body to process the intense emotions.

Sit or stand in a private, comfortable place where you feel safe and won't be disturbed.

Tense your muscles, especially in the arms, fists, jaw, and chest. Feel the tension in your body.

Open your mouth wide, as though you are about to let out a full scream, but keep your voice silent. The sensation of a scream is there, but no sound comes out.

As you "scream" silently, exhale forcefully through your mouth, pushing the air out as if you were screaming at full volume. This gives your body a release without the actual sound.

After the silent scream, slowly relax your muscles, releasing the tension in your fists, jaw, and body. Take a few deep breaths to calm down.

You can repeat this practice a few times until you feel less emotional intensity.

This practice allows the body to express the physical sensation of screaming and releasing anger, but in a quieter, more private way. It can be particularly helpful when you're in situations where you can't make noise but need to process strong feelings of anger.

Allowing Anger: Meeting It Without Resistance

Anger often carries energy that demands acknowledgment. Instead of pushing it away or acting on impulse, meeting anger with presence can create space for understanding.

Find a quiet space and bring awareness to where anger sits in your body. Notice its shape, temperature, or movement without trying to change it. Place a hand on the area, if it feels right, offering a silent acknowledgment: *I see you. You are allowed to be here.* If tension builds, take a slow breath and let the sensation exist without judgment. Stay with it for a moment, then gently shift your attention to the rest of your body, noticing that anger is present but not all-consuming.

Physical Expression: Moving with Awareness

Anger carries energy that builds in the body. Movement offers a way to release this energy without amplifying it. Instead of high-impact or competitive activities, which can escalate activation, slow, controlled movement allows anger to move through without fueling reactivity. The goal is not to overpower anger but to meet it with steady, intentional motion.

Engage in a movement that feels grounding rather than activating. Take a slow, mindful walk, feeling the weight of your steps. Try gentle stretching, noticing how your muscles respond. Flow through a few yoga poses, focusing on deep, steady breaths. If tension lingers, press your palms against a wall and push gently, feeling the energy shift. Pay attention to how each movement affects your body. Adjust as needed, staying connected to the sensations without rushing to escape them.

Disgust

Disgust is an emotional state of aversion toward something offensive. It's a message from our body that tells us something is toxic to our well-being.

Disgust says I've had it. –Jim Rohn

Disgust is the emotion that says, *this is not for me.* It shows up as an immediate wave of aversion, a pulling away in the body, a tightening in the throat, a twist in the stomach, or an instinctive desire to create distance. Disgust is a protective response that evolved to keep you safe from what feels toxic or harmful, both physically and emotionally.

Imagine picking up a grocery cart and feeling something sticky on the handle. Notice the quick recoil of your hand or the tightening in your face. Or picture opening a container in the fridge and seeing food that has clearly gone bad. Your body reacts instantly. Disgust often appears this way, as a full-body response that arrives before your thoughts have time to form.

Disgust does not show up only for sensory experiences. It also arises in response to violations of values, breaches of trust, unfair treatment, or moments that feel morally or emotionally "off." The body signals danger not through fear, but through rejection and distance.

Many people try to override disgust by minimizing it or shaming themselves for reacting. Others feel overwhelmed by how quickly and intensely it appears. But disgust is an emotion with purpose. It wants to protect you, signal your boundaries, and help you move away from what feels unsafe or incompatible with your values.

Begin by acknowledging the emotion without judgment.

I am experiencing disgust.

I feel repelled.

It is normal to feel disgust.

Everyone feels disgust sometimes.

My body is trying to protect me.

Disgust is allowed here.

Disgust often creates strong physical sensations, and soothing the body helps restore clarity. Before exploring thoughts, beliefs, or reactions, we start by steadying the nervous system and offering support to the body's immediate response.

When disgust arises, these practices help calm the intensity of the sensation and create enough space to understand what the emotion is communicating.

Helping the Body Settle

When disgust appears, the body reacts with intensity. The first step is to reduce the sensation enough to regain clarity.

If you can, pause and step away from the trigger. Let your eyes settle on something neutral. Splash cool water on your face, sip ginger ale, lean into the open freezer for a moment, or suck on peppermint. These sensory shifts help interrupt the immediate shock and give your nervous system a place to land.

If your muscles tighten, shake your hands lightly or roll your shoulders to release tension. If your breath has become shallow, lengthen your exhale and remind yourself that the reaction will pass.

Empathy

Empathy is the ability to understand and share the feelings, thoughts, or experiences of another person. It involves stepping into someone else's perspective, imagining the experience as that person, recognizing their emotions, and offering support or compassion without judgment.

Disgust often feels absolute, as if the entire experience is repelling. Empathy helps create more space inside the reaction.

Empathy for yourself is equally important. Many disgust reactions are learned responses shaped by culture, upbringing, or trauma. You may experience disgust toward your own choices, your own past, your own body, or reactions you do not understand. This is where compassion becomes vital.

You might say, *of course I feel this. My body learned this response somewhere.* Or *it makes sense that I feel repelled. I am trying to protect myself.*

Compassion transforms disgust from a rejection of yourself into a clearer message about your values, your limits, or your conditioning.

The goal is not to eliminate disgust. It is to hold it with curiosity rather than harshness.

Empathy Expansion

When disgust is tied to people or behaviors, activating empathy can reduce emotional distance and lessen judgment.

Consider what might have led to the thing you find disgusting. If it's a behavior, think about the person's experiences or motivations. If it's sensory, imagine someone who perceives it differently. How might they see it? This doesn't mean forcing yourself to accept something, just widening the lens of understanding.

Curiosity

Gently turn inward and notice if your response matches the situation. If there is a mismatch, notice the emotions underneath and tend to them. Anger often pairs with disgust.

We observe and notice beliefs, thoughts, and values as they come up, acknowledging our individual agreements and unique experiences.

We gently take mental note to explore once the physical experience of the emotion has moved through us. And continue to set them aside for now.

Offer self alternatives if possible. It is okay to meet your own needs.

Curiosity Instead of Rejection

Disgust tends to trigger avoidance. Engaging with curiosity can create a sense of control and lessen the emotional charge.

Instead of pushing away the feeling, ask small, neutral questions: *What exactly am I reacting to? What does this remind me of? Is there anything interesting about this?* Even a small shift from aversion to observation can reduce the intensity of disgust.

Mental Distancing

Disgust creates an urge to reject or push away, but mental distancing can reduce its grip by offering a more neutral perspective.

Picture the situation as if you were a scientist studying it objectively, rather than reacting personally. Imagine putting it on a screen or describing it in the most neutral language possible. If disgust feels overwhelming, remind yourself that emotions are temporary, and this reaction will pass.

Releasing the Residue

Disgust can linger even after the source is gone. Engaging in a symbolic act of cleansing can provide psychological closure.

Write down what feels repelling and then discard or destroy the paper. Visualize the disgust washing away like dirt under running water. Even something simple, like tidying a space or changing clothes, can reinforce a sense of renewal.

Allowing Preferences: Letting Yourself Be a Person With Likes and Dislikes

Many people respond to disgust with shame. They believe they should not have strong preferences, should not feel bothered, or should not react so intensely. But preferences are a natural part of being human. Disgust often highlights boundaries, values, and needs.

This exercise helps you explore your preferences without judgment.

Choose something small that brings up mild disgust or aversion. It might be a food texture, a scent, a type of humor, or a personal habit you dislike. Notice the sensation in your body. See if you can name it without criticizing it.

You might say, *my body does not prefer this. My body wants distance. This is allowed.*

Then name a preference that feels true. *I prefer warmth. I prefer clean lines. I prefer gentle voices. I prefer quieter environments. I prefer honesty. I prefer order. I prefer softness.*

Allow your body to respond. Notice how it feels to name what you do want rather than focusing only on what you do not. Preferences help anchor disgust in clarity instead of shame.

This practice teaches the nervous system that disgust is information, not a character flaw. You are allowed to have limits. You are allowed to have tastes. You are allowed to have boundaries that protect your well-being.

Surprise

Surprise is a brief emotional state responding to unexpected events in the environment. It can be perceived as positive, negative, or neutral. It's often followed by another emotion. Surprise often involves a startle response.

Surprise is the greatest gift which life can grant us. – Boris Pasternak

Surprise is a quick emotional shift, a moment when the body reacts before the mind fully understands what is happening. The heart jumps, the breath catches, and the shoulders lift. Sometimes the sensation is pleasant, like seeing an old friend or receiving unexpected good news. Other times it is jarring, like a sudden loud noise or an unforeseen change. Surprise is neither positive nor negative on its own. It is simply the body registering something unexpected.

Imagine turning a corner and nearly running into someone who appears suddenly. Feel how the body responds. A quick inhale, tightening in the chest, and widening of the eyes. Surprise moves fast because it evolved to help us reorient to new information. After the initial jolt, another emotion often follows, which may be fear, relief, amusement, frustration, or confusion.

Surprise wants to help you pay attention. It does not require immediate action. It needs grounding and a moment to let the body catch up.

Surprise often brings a startle response, and soothing the startle allows the second emotion to unfold without overwhelm.

Startle

To disturb or agitate suddenly. To start involuntarily, as from a shock of surprise or alarm.

Self soothing strategies can help to reestablish a sense of safety and calm the physiological responses of surprise.

Pause and take a moment to process the unexpected event.

Take deep breaths to calm your body, smile or laugh if the surprise is pleasant, close your eyes and count to ten if it's overwhelming, have a cup of tea or coffee, step outside for fresh air. Breathe. Enjoy a piece of chocolate or a favorite snack.

Acknowledge the unexpected moment.

Recognize and validate the physical response you are experiencing without judgment. They are a natural response to stimuli. Remember, surprise is a message from our body that tells us something is novel or different from our expectations and can be a source of excitement and growth.

I am experiencing surprise.

I am surprised.

It is normal to feel surprised.

Everyone feels surprised sometimes. Life can bring unexpected moments and events.

Notice other emotions beneath the surprise and tend to them as needed.

Laughter

Laughter, much like crying, can occur related to any of the core emotions. Who hasn't felt the terrible urge to laugh at the absolute worst time? Laughter is often linked to the unexpected, and surprise is the element of encountering something out of the ordinary.

The Incongruity Theory of Humor

This theory suggests humor comes from encountering something unexpected or incongruent with our expectations. A surprising punchline to a joke or a funny situation that unfolds differently than anticipated can trigger laughter.

Sometimes, surprise itself can be startling enough to lead to laughter. It's a way to release the built-up tension from the surprise. Imagine someone jumping out to scare you playfully, and you might end up surprised or even scared and then laughing.

Laughter is a powerful tool that can improve your health and well-being. It can relax your muscles, boost your immune system, and even help you lose weight. Laughter also has mental and social benefits. It can improve your mood, reduce stress, and strengthen your relationships.

Simulated Laughter

Relief theory posits that laughter serves as a release of psychological tension and pent-up energy. Originating from the work of thinkers like Sigmund Freud and Herbert Spencer, this theory suggests that laughter allows individuals to discharge excess nervous energy and alleviate inner psychological pressures. Freud, for example, believed that laughter helps release repressed emotions in a harmless way, providing a form of emotional catharsis.

Simulated laughter involves acting out laughter, even without feeling truly amused. It might sound silly, but research suggests the body can't fully distinguish between real and fake laughter. This means simply forcing a smile and laughter can trigger the release of feel-good endorphins and reduce stress hormones, leading to some of the same health advantages as genuine laughter. So laugh it up!

Playfulness

Playfulness can help shift emotion, offering spontaneity and flexibility when emotions feel rigid or overwhelming. Engaging in play can loosen tension and create space for curiosity.

Give yourself permission to engage in something lighthearted. This could be playing a game, doodling without a goal, trying on silly voices, or engaging in a small, playful challenge (balancing an object on your head, making up a short rhyme). The key is to focus on the experience rather than the outcome. Notice how even small moments of playfulness shift the emotional tone.

Visualization of Steadiness

Surprise can feel destabilizing, whether it's pleasant or jarring. Visualizing something steady helps the body and mind adjust to the unexpected.

Close your eyes and picture something unshakable: a deep-rooted tree, an anchor holding firm in the ocean, or a steady rhythm, like waves lapping at the shore. Breathe as you imagine its presence, allowing the image to settle in your body. If surprise feels intense, mentally step back, seeing yourself grounded in the scene rather than caught in the rush of the moment.

End Of Chapter Practice: Soothing And Responding To Core Emotions

This week you'll continue practicing soothing strategies for the emotions that arise in your day-to-day life. Using what you've explored in this chapter, begin to create a personalized plan for each of the six core emotions. Keep your focus on the felt sense in your body and your growing ability to respond, rather than react.

Practice

Start with the Body

Notice the physical sensations that signal each emotion. Is your chest tight with sadness? Does anger heat your face and clench your fists? Does surprise jolt your system? Allow the physical experience to rise without shifting immediately into story.

Create Your Plan

For each core emotion, write a brief response plan. For example:

When I feel the heat of anger, I can walk away, count to 10, breathe into my fists, or use positive self-talk.

When I feel heavy with sadness, I can cry, write, wrap myself in a blanket, or speak gently to myself.

When I feel fear, I can ground through breath, orient to safety, or move my body.

This plan can be flexible. Some strategies may help in one moment and not in another. This is practice, not perfection.

Match Strategy to Arousal State

Practice Even When Calm

Try out your strategies even when you're not overwhelmed. This builds familiarity and helps your nervous system learn new responses. Ask yourself: *What helps me feel more supported in this emotion? What does my body need when I feel this way?*

Validate the Emotion

Use affirmations and positive self-talk to normalize and validate your experience.

This is sadness. It's allowed.

Anger is a response, not a problem.

I am safe to feel my feelings.

Observe and Reflect

At the end of each day, pause to reflect:

Which emotions showed up for me?

What did my body do?

What strategy helped most?

Notice without judgment. This is learning.

By matching your response to the emotion and your nervous system state, you are building a more complete and responsive inner toolkit, one grounded in safety, flexibility, and care.

If you don't like the road you're walking, start paving another one. – Dolly Parton

You can, you should, and if you're brave enough to start, you will. – Stephen King

You're braver than you believe, and stronger than you seem, and smarter than you think. – A.A. Milne

In the midst of hate, I found there was, within me, an invincible love. In the midst of tears, I found there was, within me, an invincible smile. In the midst of chaos, I found there was, within me, an invincible calm. I realized, through it all, that in the midst of winter, I found there was, within me, an invincible summer. And that makes me happy. For it says that no matter how hard the world pushes against me, within me, there's something stronger—something better, pushing right back. – Albert Camus

Feeling the Good Stuff

I often wonder what would happen if we all spent just a few minutes a day allowing ourselves to feel in our bodies how very worthy, good enough, loved, and loveable we are RIGHT NOW, exactly as we are in this present moment. Would we all look out our windows en masse, or go outside? Feel an urge to do a kindness for another? Indulge in our unique creativity? Turn on music and dance around our kitchens?

Meet yourself where you are right now with love. – Tiffany Todd, LCSW

Objective: Learn somatic and non-somatic strategies for the emotion of enjoyment.

Enjoyment

An emotional state of enjoyment, ranging in intensity from mild contentment to deep joy. It usually arises from meaningful connection, accomplishment, or the simple pleasures of the present moment. It draws us closer to what feels safe or satisfying.

When you climb a beautiful mountain, invite your child within to climb with you. When you contemplate the sunset, invite her to enjoy it with you. – Thich Nhat Hanh, *Reconciliation: Healing the Inner Child*

Enjoyment often appears as warmth, brightness, or a sense of lightness moving through the body. It may feel like a soft glow in the chest, a spontaneous smile, or the simple ease of being fully in the present moment. Imagine sunlight on your skin, laughing with someone you trust, or tasting something you love. Notice how your body responds. Perhaps your breath deepens, your shoulders loosen, or an easiness comes into your face. Enjoyment expands you from the inside, inviting you toward what feels nourishing.

Begin by acknowledging the experience with kindness.

I am experiencing enjoyment.

I am enjoying this moment.

I am allowed to enjoy my present moment.

It is safe to feel enjoyment.

It is normal to feel enjoyment.

Everyone experiences enjoyment sometimes.

Life can bring moments of happiness and delight.

Enjoyment is an emotion that arises when something feels good, meaningful, or fulfilling. It helps you connect with the richness of life and the things your senses prefer. Yet many people struggle to stay with enjoyment. Some rush past it quickly. Others feel undeserving of happiness. For many, joy feels unfamiliar or even uncomfortable, especially if their nervous system is used to being on alert or shut down.

Enjoyment, like every emotion, simply wants to be felt. It asks for presence. It asks for savoring. It offers grounding, connection, and resilience when we allow it to move through the body.

The Felt Sense Of Enjoyment

Enjoyment expands. It lightens the body, lifts the chest, and invites movement. At its most subtle, it's a soft warmth. At its peak, it's full-body radiance.

Enjoyment and Hyperarousal

When enjoyment shifts into hyperarousal, the body becomes highly energized and ready to engage fully in the experience. This can feel like excitement, exhilaration, or an overflow of positive energy. There may be a quickening heartbeat, brighter breath, warmth spreading through the body, and an eagerness to laugh, move, or share.

Hyperarousal can feel good, but it can also slip into dysregulation.

Enjoyment may tip into restlessness, impulsivity, or difficulty slowing down. The body may feel overstimulated, jittery, or scattered. Thoughts may race. There may be pressure to keep the good feeling going, to do more, say more, or hold on tightly to the pleasurable experience. The nervous system becomes charged in a way that feels less like joy and more like urgency.

In this state, enjoyment can feel overwhelming. The nervous system is activated, creating a buzz that edges toward chaos instead of connection. The joy is real, but the grounding may be missing.

Enjoyment and Hypoarousal

When enjoyment slips into hypoarousal, the body responds with quietness or a muted sense of contentment. The experience becomes more internal and subdued, marked by gentle warmth, soft breath, and relaxed muscles.

But hypoarousal can also dampen enjoyment so much that it becomes hard to feel at all.

Pleasure may feel distant or muted. The body may feel heavy or disconnected, as if the joy is trapped behind glass. You may know something is supposed to feel good but cannot fully access the sensation. There may be numbness, flatness, or a sense of being emotionally unplugged from the moment.

In this state, the nervous system has shifted too far toward shutdown. Enjoyment is present in theory, but the body does not rise to meet it. The spark of pleasure is there, but the nervous system is too subdued to amplify it.

Somatic Practice: Holding Joy Without Shrinking or Chasing

This practice teaches the nervous system how to contain enjoyment gently, whether you tend to block it, chase it or would like to expand it.

Find a comfortable seat or lie down. Let your breath settle. Bring to mind a small enjoyable moment. Not something huge. Something simple. A warm drink. A color you love. A memory of laughter. Notice the first small sensation of enjoyment in your body, maybe a soft lift in your chest or a gentle warmth behind your ribs.

Place one hand over the area where you feel the sensation. You are not trying to make it bigger or smaller. You are practicing containment. Breathe slowly into your hand, as if your breath is creating a soft boundary around the feeling. If the joy tries to swell too quickly, let your hand become a steady container. If the joy tries to disappear, let your hand be a place the feeling can return to.

Say softly inside yourself, *I can hold a little joy. I do not need to chase it. I do not need to shrink it. I can stay here.*

Take two or three more breaths with your hand on your body. If your attention wavers, simply return to the warmth of your palm. When the practice feels complete, allow the sensation to rest where it is. You are teaching your nervous system that joy can rise and settle inside you without needing to run from it or cling to it.

Framing Enjoyment Within The Window Of Tolerance

Whether felt in a more active or subdued way, enjoyment within the window of tolerance brings a sense of fulfillment and well-being. It can be experienced fully without overwhelming the body or slipping into shutdown.

In hyperarousal, enjoyment can be gently tempered to prevent it from becoming too overstimulating. Breathing and grounding exercises help anchor the experience while still embracing the joy.

In hypoarousal, the focus is on staying connected to the pleasant sensations without numbing or disconnecting. Gentle movement or mindfulness keeps the experience alive and present.

When enjoyment is felt within this window, it becomes a nourishing force. It strengthens our ability to connect with others, savor life's moments, and foster resilience in the face of stress.

Regulating Hyperarousal

To bring enjoyment back to balance when it tips into hyperarousal, calming techniques like deep breathing or grounding help to maintain the connection without overwhelming the nervous system. Imagine slowing down, savoring the joy rather than rushing through it. Allow what feels right to you, there is no right or wrong way to feel enjoyment.

Where focus goes, energy flows. – Tony Robbins

Dance and Music

We have to dance it out. – Meredith Grey, Grey's Anatomy

The cast of *Grey's Anatomy* danced their way through the chaos, grief, relief, anger, and joy, using movement to process the emotional rollercoaster that defined their lives. Dance and music offer this same outlet. They can help us move emotion through the body, settle into what we feel, or meet intensity with intentional expression. They can also amplify and deepen the experience of enjoyment, allowing joy to expand beyond the mind and fully inhabit the body.

Dance meets the nervous system differently depending on the state you are in. When joy rises quickly and becomes bright, fast, or hard to contain, movement can help direct that intensity into something intentional rather than letting it swell unchecked. In hyperarousal, the goal is not to amplify the excitement but to give it a shape. Choosing music with a steady rhythm and allowing your body to move with deliberate weight can help the energy travel downward instead of spiraling upward. You might notice your feet grounding you as you step, or the sense of your body reclaiming a steady rhythm. Dance becomes a container that guides the excess joy into movement that feels expressive rather than overwhelming. If the music pushes you toward even more activation, slowing your motions or choosing calmer songs can bring you back toward steadiness.

In hypoarousal, dance takes on a different role. When enjoyment feels muted or far away, gentle movement can help bring warmth and aliveness back into the body. The intention is not to force big expressions but to invite small motions that begin to wake you from the inside. A slow sway, the soft rolling of your shoulders, or a subtle shift of weight can create a gradual sense of engagement. Sometimes a single note or familiar melody is enough to stir something within you, reminding your body of what it feels like to participate in joy. Movement becomes an invitation rather than a demand, a slow warming instead of a sudden surge.

When the body is within the window of tolerance, dance and music can deepen enjoyment in a grounded and expansive way. Music carries the emotional tone, and upbeat rhythms, energetic melodies, or soaring harmonies naturally invite the body into motion, amplifying the sensations of enjoyment. A favorite song can shift energy instantly, sparking movement that feels effortless and alive. The body responds with lightness, arms reaching outward, steps bouncing, laughter moving through you without planning or thought. In these moments, dance becomes an expression of pure joy that reinforces and extends the feeling rather than letting it fade too quickly.

Even small movements, such as a sway, a tap of the foot, or a gentle rocking, can enhance enjoyment by bringing more presence to the moment. Dancing in a group or with a partner adds another layer, the synchrony of movement creating a sense of connection and shared happiness. Joy often becomes contagious, moving between bodies and strengthening the nervous system's ability to hold pleasure.

By letting go of inhibition, choosing music that resonates with your internal state, and allowing your body to respond naturally, enjoyment can deepen from a fleeting sensation into something embodied and sustained. Reflection afterward, whether through stillness, journaling, or simply savoring the afterglow, reinforces the body's capacity to hold joy, making it more accessible in everyday life.

Playful Exaggeration

Enjoyment can sometimes feel overwhelming in hyperarousal, making it hard to settle into the experience. Leaning into playfulness through exaggerated facial expressions, movements, or storytelling can help channel the energy into joy rather than restlessness.

Pick a positive moment or experience and describe it with over-the-top enthusiasm, big gestures, animated voice, or exaggerated expressions. If moving, try bouncing slightly or playfully overemphasizing your motions.

Grounded Joy

When enjoyment becomes hard to contain, return to the edges of your body. Press your feet into the floor. Hold something warm or solid. Place one hand on your chest. These grounding cues create containment so the joy can be held rather than pursued. You are not dampening the emotion. You are giving it a place to land.

The Gentle Pause

Create a small pause after an enjoyable moment. One slow breath. One moment of stillness. A quiet reflection such as, *this was good.* The pause teaches the nervous system that joy can end without collapse, and that grounding does not mean losing the pleasure. The joy can stay with you, even as you move back into your day.

Regulating Hypoarousal

When enjoyment feels muted or distant, gentle activation techniques like stretching or engaging the senses can help reawaken the body's capacity to experience pleasure. Something as simple as tuning into the warmth of sunlight or the taste of a favorite treat can bring enjoyment back to the surface, allowing it to be felt more deeply.

Glimmers

tiny micro moments of joy.

Glimmer is a term coined by Deb Dana, a licensed clinical social worker specializing in complex trauma and the polyvagal theory. It refers to small, fleeting moments of joy, peace, safety, or connection. These moments can be simple and seemingly insignificant, but they have a powerful impact on our nervous system.

Glimmer moments help signal our nervous system to switch from a stressed or threatened state to a safe and social state. This allows us to feel calmer, more regulated, and more connected to ourselves and others.

A glimmer can be anything that sparks a positive feeling.

Glimmers can be found anywhere, in any moment. Children are much more inclined toward stopping to plunge their hands into the mud and tromp through rain puddles. They notice everything that is going on around them and want to point out all the things they have noticed to their caregivers.

Be like a child and notice a brilliant color you've never seen quite like that before. Listen to the bird's song that catches your ear and stay with it just a moment longer than you normally would. Yell "cow" loudly in the car on road trips whenever you spot one. Stop in the dusty museum and explore for a few hours. Observe the geese on the roof across the way. Indulge your curiosity and sense of wonder at this endlessly fascinating present moment.

How to Cultivate Glimmer Moments

Practice Mindfulness: Pay attention to your daily experiences without judgment. What sights, sounds, smells, or sensations bring you a sense of calm or joy?

Keep a Gratitude Journal: Taking a few minutes each day to reflect on things you're grateful for can cultivate a more positive outlook and heighten your awareness of positive experiences.

Engage in Activities You Enjoy: Make time for hobbies or activities that bring you pleasure.

Connect with Others: Spend time with loved ones who make you feel supported and understood.

Spend Time in Nature: Nature has a calming effect on the nervous system. Go for a walk in the park, sit by a stream, or simply gaze at the clouds.

Savoring Small Pleasures

Hypoarousal can dull enjoyment, making pleasure feel distant. Deliberately stretching out a moment of enjoyment helps awaken the senses.

Choose a simple enjoyable experience, such as sipping a warm drink, feeling the sun on your skin, or listening to a favorite song. Pause to notice every detail: temperature, texture, movement, sound. Name three things you appreciate about the moment before moving on.

Joyful Micro-Movements

Hypoarousal can make engagement feel like effort. Small, intentional movements help bridge the gap between stillness and full participation in pleasure.

If dancing feels like too much, start with tapping your fingers or swaying gently. If smiling feels distant, try a soft half-smile. Let the movement be as small as needed to invite connection to enjoyment.

Micro-Savoring

Begin with the smallest sensation of joy you can find. The lift at the corners of your mouth. A gentle warmth in your chest. A softening around your eyes. Stay with that sensation for one inhale, then release it if you need to. Over time, one breath becomes two. This practice teaches the nervous system that joy can be held in tiny, safe amounts.

Permission Phrases

Offer your body explicit reassurance.

It is safe to feel this.

I can let in a small amount.

This feeling is allowed.

Enhancing Enjoyment

Sharing and Celebrating to Deepen Enjoyment

Joy has a unique way of expanding when shared. When we invite others into our moments of celebration, we allow joy to ripple outward, creating a sense of connection and belonging. Whether it's a small achievement or a significant life event, sharing with others magnifies the experience, turning fleeting moments of happiness into lasting memories.

Celebrating with others, whether through a meal, a conversation, or a shared activity, allows us to witness the happiness reflected in the faces of those around us. This mutual exchange of joy creates a feedback loop, where each person's enjoyment builds upon the other's, deepening the overall experience.

When someone honors you by sharing their joy, respond as if it is your own. Hold it as precious.

Even small gestures, like telling a friend about something that made you smile, or marking a personal milestone with someone who understands its significance, can transform a private moment into a communal one. This act of sharing enhances our capacity for enjoyment by bringing others into the joy, reminding us that happiness grows when nurtured together.

When we celebrate with others, we're not only acknowledging the moment itself but also the relationships that enrich our lives. This creates a sense of gratitude, further amplifying the pleasure and meaning of the experience. In this way, joy becomes something not just experienced, but truly lived and shared.

Gentle Presence With Pleasure

When joy feels steady and grounded, you can deepen the experience by turning your attention toward how the sensation lives in your body.

Begin by noticing where the enjoyment rests. It may feel like warmth in your chest, a lightness in your face, or a soft opening in your breath. Stay with the sensation and allow it to unfold without rushing it or trying to make it more than it is.

Let your breath move slowly and naturally. As you inhale, notice how the emotion shifts or expands. As you exhale, feel your body soften around it. You are not trying to hold the feeling tightly. You are letting it sit beside you like a familiar companion. If your mind wanders, gently return to the physical sensation and to the way your body responds. This presence strengthens the nervous system's capacity to hold pleasure and teaches your body that joy can remain without slipping into urgency or fading too quickly.

Gratitude Noticing

Gratitude begins with noticing one small thing that feels good in this moment.

Let your eyes rest on something comforting or pleasing. It may be the color of a blanket, the curve of a mug, the sound of a familiar voice, or the way light moves across a nearby surface. Pause for a breath and let yourself feel what is pleasant about it.

Name quietly to yourself what you appreciate. It can be as simple as saying, I like this color, or, This reminds me I am safe. Gratitude becomes a gentle doorway into enjoyment, helping the body recognize moments of ease without requiring the emotion to grow or perform.

You do not need to force positivity, only to allow the smallest spark of appreciation to settle in your body and expand your connection to the present moment.

Trauma's Impact On Enjoyment

Trauma, especially when ongoing or severe, can create a sense of disconnection from enjoyment. When the body is primed for survival, whether stuck in a state of hyperarousal, constantly on edge, or in hypoarousal, feeling numb or detached, pleasure can feel inaccessible. The mind may scan for danger instead of allowing ease, or moments of joy may feel fleeting, unfamiliar, or even unsafe.

Joy Beside Pain

Enjoyment does not demand that everything in your life feel good. Many people hesitate to feel joy when they are grieving, stressed, or carrying unspoken heaviness. Others feel a quiet guilt when they experience something warm or beautiful while the world around them suffers. The nervous system may treat joy as something dangerous, indulgent, or unfair, as if letting yourself feel good means you are ignoring what is hard.

But joy is not a denial of pain. It does not erase your awareness or your care. Joy and sorrow live in the same human body, and both emotions have purpose. Joy reminds you of your capacity to feel, to connect, and to soften. Pain reminds you of what is important to you and you are allowed to hold both.

If guilt or resistance arises when joy appears, notice where it lands in your body. Maybe your chest tightens or your breath shortens. Perhaps your mind quickly scans for reasons you should not feel this good. Instead of pushing the joy away, offer yourself a quiet internal reminder: *Joy does not mean the pain is gone. Both are allowed here.*

You can care about suffering and still allow yourself one small moment of ease. You can grieve and still feel a spark of laughter. You can be healing and still feel warmth in your chest when something good touches you. Joy is not betrayal. It is a resource that strengthens your ability to stay present with what is difficult.

Let joy and pain sit beside each other, neither cancelling the other out. This coexistence expands your capacity to feel the fullness of your humanity, not just the parts that ache.

Future Emotional Experience Practice

As your nervous system builds capacity for enjoyment in the present, you can also begin to explore what it feels like to imagine a future that is safe, steady, and fulfilling. This next practice is about letting your body briefly experience sensations of relief, joy, and contentment, as if more of what you need is already here.

You can always adjust the visualization to match what feels possible for you right now.

Find a comfortable space where you can be at ease and undisturbed. Sit or lie down, allowing your body to relax. Close your eyes and take a few deep, calming breaths. With each breath, feel your body settling deeper into the present moment. Let your shoulders drop, your jaw soften, and your body begin to settle.

Set the intention to imagine a version of your life where what you have long needed or hoped for is present. Not perfect, but supportive, meaningful, and enough.

Begin to visualize yourself in a place that makes you feel at ease. It could be your home, a peaceful retreat, or somewhere familiar where you feel safe and calm. Notice the details of this space. What do you see? What sounds surround you? Are there any familiar or soothing scents in the air? Allow yourself to settle into this imagined place.

Now, imagine that some of what you have longed for is here. There may be a sense of stability, of being supported in your day-to-day life. Your relationships may feel more connected, more understanding. There may be a sense of alignment in how you move through your day, a feeling that things are more manageable, more steady.

Let yourself feel the impact of this. Notice what begins to arise within you.

A sense of relief may begin to move through your body, like a soft exhale you didn't realize you were holding. Joy might show up as warmth or lightness, spreading gently through your chest or face. Gratitude may feel expansive, like something opening or softening inside. Contentment might settle as a steady, grounded feeling, like your body can finally rest.

As these sensations arise, bring your attention to how they feel in your body. Notice where they begin, how they move, and whether they shift or deepen. Let yourself stay with these sensations, even if they are subtle.

Notice the emotions available to you now.

Take a moment to remain with this experience. With each breath, allow the sensations to continue in a way that feels natural. There is no need to force anything. Simply notice what is present.

If you notice any resistance or hesitation, gently acknowledge it. This is a natural response. Notice where it shows up in your body and allow it to be there as well, without needing to change it.

Place one hand over your heart and the other on your stomach if that feels supportive. Feel the rise and fall of your breath, anchoring yourself in this moment. Allow the sensations of ease, relief, or steadiness to move gently through your body.

When you feel ready, begin to bring your awareness back to the present moment. Notice the space around you, the surface beneath you, and the feeling of your body here. The sensations you experienced may linger, even as the visualization comes to a close. You can return to this practice whenever you need to, continuing to build familiarity with these experiences in your body.

End Of Chapter Practice: Explore An Emotion You Enjoy

Find a comfortable seated position or lie down. Take a few deep breaths, allowing your body to settle into the present moment. Let your mind gently focus on the experience ahead.

Think of an emotion that brings you joy, peace, or contentment. Perhaps it's happiness, excitement, love, or calmness. Whatever comes to mind, allow it to be your focus.

Now, begin to notice where this emotion lives in your body. Does it feel expansive, endless, or sparkly? Warm, tingly, or cozy? Does your body feel energized or calm, charged or relaxed? Lean into these sensations, letting them grow a little bit stronger. Imagine the emotion is radiating from your chest, your stomach, or wherever you feel it most strongly.

Engage Your Senses

Imagine if this emotion had a color. What color would it be? Is it bright or soft, warm or cool?

If the emotion had a texture, would it feel light and airy, or soft and smooth? Let your mind explore these qualities without judgment.

Can you hear any sounds associated with this feeling?

Is there a scent or taste that accompanies this emotion?

Movement or Stillness

As you focus on this emotion, notice how your body responds. Do you feel a natural urge to move, perhaps to sway or stretch? Or do you feel a sense of stillness and groundedness? Honor what your body wants to do. You might move gently or remain still, noticing the energy flowing through you.

Bring in a Memory or Visualization

Recall a memory or imagine a situation that evokes this emotion.

Where are you?

Who's around you?

What sights, sounds, or smells surround you?

Visualize the scene clearly, allowing yourself to feel the emotion growing stronger as the memory or imagined situation unfolds.

Embrace Any Resistance

If you notice resistance, perhaps a sense of stuckness, doubt, or discomfort, approach it with curiosity and kindness. Remember, resistance is a natural part of the process, especially if you're accustomed to focusing on challenges or negative emotions. Validate these feelings without judgment, offering yourself reassurance that it's safe to feel good.

Expand the Feeling

Now, gently breathe into the sensation of this emotion.

With each inhale, allow the feeling to grow a little bit more, filling your chest or wherever you feel it strongest.

With each exhale, let any resistance or stuckness dissolve.

Can you hold onto this feeling for another breath?

Validate and Stay Present

Remind yourself that it is safe to feel this emotion. You are allowed to feel joy, happiness, or contentment. Let yourself sit with the sensation, even if it feels new or a bit unfamiliar. Can you lean just a tiny bit more into this emotion, expanding your capacity to hold onto it? Stay with it for just a moment longer.

Extend the Practice

Challenge yourself to carry this feeling with you throughout the day, returning to the physical sensations whenever you need a boost. Notice if you can approach your interactions and activities with a greater sense of the emotion you cultivated.

Reflect on the Experience

As you gently bring yourself back to the present moment, take note of how this exercise felt.

Did you learn anything new about your body's response to this emotion?

How did it feel to stay with the emotion a bit longer?

What sensations stood out to you?

How did it feel to intentionally cultivate and amplify these sensations?

What, if anything, surprised you about this experience?

Remember, you can revisit this practice anytime you need to reconnect with the emotions that bring you joy, peace, and a sense of well-being. The more you practice, the easier it becomes to shift your focus toward the good, creating a more positive and fulfilling experience.

Thoughts: Explore and Investigate Nonjudgmentally

Objective: Explore and identify negative beliefs about self, others and the world.

When we recognize that we have a habit of replaying old events and reacting to new events as if they were the old ones, we can begin to notice when that habit energy comes up. We can then gently remind ourselves that we have another choice. We can look at the moment as it is, a fresh moment, and leave the past for a time when we can look at it compassionately. – Thich Nhat Hanh,

It's in my head, it's in my head
Running around up there again
Stuck in my head, it's in my head
Running around. – Panda Bear, "Never Ending Game"

Thoughts

Thought

An idea or opinion formed in the mind.

Belief

Something that is accepted, considered to be true, or held as an opinion.

Thoughts become a frame of reference for the world around us.

Up until now, we've focused on emotions as they arise in the body, how they move, settle, and shift. But emotions don't exist in isolation. They are shaped by the meaning we give them, the interpretations we attach to them, and the patterns of thought that influence our responses.

Thoughts act as a bridge between sensation and action. They help us make sense of experience, offering a way to organize emotions and decide how to respond. But not all thoughts are neutral. Some thoughts become deeply ingrained beliefs about who we are, how others see us, and what we can expect from the world. These beliefs, formed early and reinforced over time, can become a filter for every experience, distorting our perspective, keeping us stuck in familiar patterns.

Thoughts as Amplifiers

When we are outside our window of tolerance, our thoughts tend to loop, often amplifying the emotions we feel. This creates a feedback loop where the more we think about a situation, the more intense our emotional response becomes.

For instance, thoughts like *I should have handled that differently,* or *why do I always say things like that?* keep us stuck in the emotion and even amplify it. Our rumination makes it difficult for the nervous system to return to a regulated state, because it amplifies feelings of guilt, shame, or fear.

When you notice negative intrusive thoughts, let that be a cue to pause rather than engage. These thoughts often arise when your nervous system has moved outside of its window of tolerance. Instead of debating or analyzing them right away, gently set them to the side and turn your attention toward regulating your body first.

Intrusive thoughts frequently carry a negative bias and tend to reflect unpreferred beliefs formed during earlier emotional experiences. When the system is activated, those beliefs can feel louder and more convincing. But thoughts that arise in dysregulation are not always accurate reflections of the present moment.

Thoughts we repeatedly entertain and interact with strengthen the beliefs we hold about ourselves, others, and the world. Gentle attention creates the internal steadiness needed before examining or reshaping those beliefs.

How to know if a thought is helpful or unhelpful

A thought is **helpful** if it creates clarity, expands perspective, or guides effective action. You can often feel this in the body. Helpful thoughts tend to bring a sense of ease, steadiness, or relief, even when facing challenges. For example, *I made a mistake, but I can learn from it* might bring a small exhale, a loosening in the chest, or a feeling of possibility.

A thought is **unhelpful** if it reinforces negative schemas, fuels distress, or disconnects from present reality. These thoughts often trigger tension, constriction, or agitation in the body. *I failed, so I will always fail.* It might bring a sinking heaviness, a tightening in the throat, or a rush of anxiety.

To assess a thought, notice.

What does my body do when I think this? Does it tense, collapse, or brace? Or does it settle, soften, or expand?

What emotion arises with this thought? Does it bring clarity and movement, or does it keep me stuck in shame, fear, or hopelessness?

Is this thought supporting safety, or is it amplifying distress? If a thought tightens the body and fuels overwhelm, it may be unhelpful. If it allows for breath, grounding, or a sense of possibility, it's likely more aligned with the present moment.

Creating Distance from Unhelpful Thoughts

Notice the thought. Bring awareness to the unhelpful thought without trying to change it. Simply observe: *What is my mind saying?*

Label It. Instead of identifying with the thought, reframe it as an event: *I am having the thought that...* This creates space between you and the thought.

Engage the Senses. Shift focus to your surroundings. Name three things you see, hear, and feel. This anchors you in the present.

Visualize the Thought Floating Away. Imagine placing the thought on a leaf in a stream, a cloud in the sky, or writing it in sand as a wave washes it away.

Reconnect with the Body. Take a slow breath or move in a way that feels grounding, reminding yourself that thoughts are just thoughts, not absolute truths.

This practice helps loosen the grip of unpreferred thoughts, allowing for more clarity and choice in how you respond.

From Thoughts To Beliefs

To create lasting change, we must look beyond moment-to-moment thoughts and examine the deeper structures that shape our emotional world. The beliefs that underlie persistent emotional patterns, how they form, how they shape behavior, and how shifting them can open new possibilities for experiencing self and others.

As you've moved through this process, you may have noticed patterns in your thoughts, recurring themes about yourself, others, or the world. Some of these thoughts may point to deeper, underlying beliefs that shape how you experience emotions.

Beliefs About Self, Others, and the World

What does this experience that I am having say about me as a person?

What meaning am I giving this experience?

Repetitive, intrusive negative thoughts often trace back to core beliefs formed in early development. These beliefs shape how we see ourselves, relationships, and the world. They often take the form of *I am* statements.

I am not safe.

I am not good enough.

I cannot depend on others for help.

These beliefs don't arise in isolation, they're rooted in the emotional environment we grew up in. The beliefs come from how caregivers responded to our emotions, what they taught us about connection, and how we learned to see ourselves in relation to others.

Francine Shapiro, creator of EMDR, identified several common themes of negative beliefs that tend to organize around four core areas.

Responsibility

It's my fault. I am not good enough. Something is wrong with me. I am a burden. I am not worthy.

These beliefs stem from internalized shame, self-blame, or the sense that one must carry the burden for what goes wrong or the emotional state of another. Often rooted in environments where mistakes were met with criticism, care was conditional, or emotional needs were unmet, these beliefs create a deep fear of failure and a tendency toward perfectionism or over-responsibility. The body may hold these beliefs as tightness in the chest, a heavy sense of pressure, or a persistent inner tension, as if bracing for judgment.

Safety / Vulnerability

I am not safe. I cannot protect myself. I cannot trust anyone.

These beliefs stem from experiences where danger, real or perceived, felt unpredictable or inescapable. They are often rooted in environments where emotional or physical safety was compromised, leading to chronic hypervigilance, fear, or difficulty trusting others. The body may hold these beliefs as tension through the shoulders or jaw, a scanning quality in the eyes, restlessness, or a persistent sense of unease.

Control / Choice

I have no control. I am powerless. I must please everyone. My needs don't matter.

These beliefs develop when a person has repeatedly felt helpless, unheard, or at the mercy of others' needs and expectations. The beliefs can lead to patterns of passivity, perfectionism, or people-pleasing as a way to regain a sense of stability. The body may respond with heaviness, collapse through the chest or posture, tightness in the chest, or difficulty asserting boundaries.

Connection / Belonging

I don't belong. I am unimportant. I will always be rejected. I am too much. I don't matter.

These beliefs are rooted in early experiences of exclusion, neglect, or inconsistent emotional attunement. They create a deep fear of abandonment or invisibility, making relationships feel uncertain or conditional. The body may hold these beliefs as social withdrawal, a constricted throat, a pulling inward through the chest, or a deep ache of loneliness.

Perhaps newly formed self had a caregiver who hovered, solved, and jumped in whenever they struggled. Over time, they may have internalized the belief: *I must be incapable, why else would they not trust me to do things myself?*

Or maybe newly formed self grew up in a family where a sibling required extra care. *Others don't care about my needs. I do not matter unless I take care of others. Love must be earned through self-sacrifice.*

Or perhaps newly formed self had caregivers whose reactions were oversized and unpredictable. *I am not safe. Something must be wrong with me.*

Generalization of Beliefs

Once established, beliefs spread beyond the original experience, shaping thoughts, emotions, and behaviors across different areas of life. This can lead to distorted thoughts.

Overgeneralization: *I failed this task, so I fail at everything.*

Catastrophizing: *If I make a mistake, everything will fall apart.*

Selective Attention: Only noticing experiences that reinforce the belief while ignoring evidence to the contrary.

These patterns create self-fulfilling prophecies. If someone believes *I am unlovable,* they may avoid connection, reinforcing isolation. If someone believes *I am powerless,* they may hesitate to assert themselves, reinforcing helplessness.

Because beliefs are reinforced through repeated emotional and physiological experiences, they can be difficult to shift through thinking alone. The body plays a critical role in sustaining these patterns.

Bottom-up approaches work by shifting how these beliefs are stored in the body. When the body experiences safety, beliefs loosen, making space for new perspectives. The goal isn't just to think differently but to feel differently, to embody new ways of experiencing self, others, and the world.

Is This an Activated Belief?

When emotions shift suddenly, ask yourself: *What belief about self, others, or the world is being activated? What does this experience that I am having say about me as a person?*

If frustration with a partner triggers deep fear, perhaps the belief *I am unlovable* is at play. If anger rises when someone challenges you, it may stem from a belief about being unheard. Recognizing the belief beneath the emotion makes the response understandable and make sense.

These beliefs may feel less real when you're calm, but that doesn't mean they don't hold weight in moments of activation. Some part of you, often the child within, still carries them. There's no right or wrong intensity, no need to rush the process.

If beliefs feel overwhelming, it may indicate the need for more regulation and safety-building before deeper exploration. Start by noticing patterns with curiosity, like an investigator piecing together meaning.

What triggered this emotional response?

When have I felt this way before?

What does this experience seem to say about me?

We are not forcing change, we are increasing understanding. When emotions and beliefs are brought into awareness, their grip begins to loosen, creating space for something new.

Before exploring the six core emotions, it can help to understand one crucial idea: Emotions make sense when you understand the belief attached to them. A belief is like a lens your nervous system learned to look through. When it gets activated, it can tint the entire present moment, often without you realizing it. The emotion is real, the body's signals are real, and the belief is trying to explain those signals based on what it learned long ago. When the belief becomes visible, the emotional response becomes understandable rather than overwhelming.

Beliefs And The Core Emotions

In the chapters leading up to this one, you have been practicing how to notice emotions, name physical sensations, and gently observe the thoughts that follow. Now we return to the six core emotions — fear, anger, sadness, disgust, surprise, and enjoyment — but this time through the lens of belief.

The body is always reading the world. The body constantly scans sensory cues, posture, facial expression, tone of voice, and more. When your nervous system detects something familiar, it not only activates an emotion, it often turns on an entire network of learning that includes images, sensations, urges, and core beliefs.

For example, a raised voice might bring a tight chest and heat in the face. The body labels this as anger or fear. At the same time, old beliefs may light up. *I am in trouble. I am not safe. No one hears me.* In this way, emotions and beliefs are intertwined. The body responds first. The belief steps forward to explain what it means.

You do not have to sort all of this out at once. You are using the same steps you already know: recognize, validate, allow, soothe, and then gently wonder about meaning. First you recognize the physical sensations. Then you connect those sensations to an emotion. You acknowledge and validate the emotion. You allow and soothe the body first. Only then do you begin to explore what beliefs may have been activated.

Below are common belief themes that often arise with each core emotion. They are not rules, only possibilities. You may recognize yourself in some and not in others. That is information, not a problem. In the next chapter, you will begin to experiment with preferred beliefs. For now, your only task is to notice what seems to be here already.

Fear

In the body, fear may feel like a racing heart, shallow breath, trembling, tension, or feeling frozen or on high alert.

Fear is the body's way of signaling possible danger. Even when there is no immediate threat, old fear networks can be activated by familiar cues, pulling forward beliefs that once helped you survive.

Common belief themes with fear include thoughts like: *I am not safe. Something bad is about to happen. I cannot handle this. I am alone and no one will help me. The world is dangerous and unpredictable.*

After you have grounded and soothed the body, you can ask yourself whether there is real danger here right now, or whether your body is remembering something from another time. You might notice whether the belief matches the present, or whether it feels like it belongs to an earlier chapter of your life. Fear makes sense when you look at what your nervous system has lived through. You are not arguing with your body's history, only beginning to notice when the past is coloring the present.

Sadness

In the body, sadness may feel like heaviness, sinking, a tight throat, tears, or an urge to withdraw or slow down.

Sadness often arises when the body recognizes loss, change, or disconnection. Alongside the heaviness, old beliefs about worth, needs, and being cared for may come online.

Common belief themes with sadness include thoughts such as: *My needs are a burden. I am too much. No one will stay if I show how I feel. I will always be left or forgotten. What I want/feel does not matter.*

After soothing your nervous system, you might wonder what story about you seems to come with this sadness. You can ask yourself whether you learned somewhere that your sadness was unwanted or unsafe. The goal is understanding, not forcing a new belief.

Anger

In the body, anger may feel like heat, pressure, clenched muscles, a surge of energy, or a strong urge to act or speak.

Anger often appears when the body notices a boundary crossed, a need ignored, or an injustice uncorrected. Along with the felt sense of anger, certain beliefs may activate, especially if similar needs in the past were not heard or respected.

Common belief themes with anger include ideas such as: *My needs do not matter. No one listens to me. I have to fight to be heard. If I do not stand up for myself, I will be walked over. Other people will not respect me unless I push back hard. It is not safe to express my needs.*

Once your body has settled back toward your window of tolerance, you might gently ask yourself what this anger seems to say about you, about others, or about the world. You can also wonder whether the belief that shows up fits the present moment, or whether it feels older than this situation. You are not trying to influence the belief yet. You are simply noticing how your anger and the belief make sense together.

Disgust

In the body, disgust may feel like curling away, tightening in the stomach or throat, a sense of repulsion, or a sharp urge to reject.

Disgust often protects you from what feels toxic, unsafe, or out of alignment with your values. It can arise in response to physical stimuli but also social stimuli.

Common belief themes with disgust include thoughts such as: *I have no choices. I have no control. I must get away from this or I will be contaminated or harmed. People who do this are bad or dangerous. If I were truly good, I would never feel or do anything like this. Parts of me are unacceptable or dirty. I am only safe if I avoid anything that reminds me of this.*

After the intensity of the sensation has eased, you might ask whether your disgust is protecting you from real harm, or whether it is tied to old rules and shame. You can notice whether you are turning this feeling only outward toward others, or also inward toward yourself. You can honor disgust as a signal while also becoming curious about whether the belief attached to it still fits who you are now.

Surprise

In the body, surprise may feel like a quick intake of breath, widened eyes, a sudden jolt or startle, or a brief spike of energy.

Surprise is the body's response to the unexpected. It can be pleasant, unpleasant, or neutral. When surprise is paired with past unpredictability, criticism, or chaos, certain beliefs may activate.

Common belief themes with surprise include ideas such as: *I must always be prepared or something will go wrong. If I am caught off guard, I will be shamed or hurt. I cannot relax because anything could happen. I am not safe unless I am in control. Other people's choices are dangerous or unpredictable.*

After your nervous system settles from the startle, you might wonder what this surprise seems to say about you or your safety. You can ask yourself whether you feel like you should have seen this coming, even if that was impossible. Surprise itself is brief. What often lingers is the belief that is turned on in its wake.

Enjoyment

In the body, enjoyment may feel like warmth, lightness, expansion, ease in the breath, a softening in the face, or a bright, activated energy.

Enjoyment can feel simple, but for many people it is complicated. When joy arises, belief networks may activate that question whether feeling good is safe or allowed.

Common belief themes with enjoyment include ideas such as: *I do not deserve to feel this good. If I relax, something bad will happen. Other people will be upset if I am happy. It is selfish to enjoy myself when others are struggling. Good things never last, so I should not get attached.*

After noticing and savoring the physical sensations of enjoyment, you might gently ask what makes it hard to let yourself feel this fully. You can notice whether any beliefs show up that tell you to shut this down or move on quickly. Your task is not to force joy to stay, only to notice when old beliefs try to pull you away from it.

Consistency

You can keep returning to these questions slowly, in small doses, after you regulate. The point is not to correct yourself, but to understand the link between what your body feels and what you have learned to believe.

Remember that the most important aspect of this process is developing self-compassion and patience as you learn to navigate your emotional landscape. There will be times when you fall back into old patterns of suppressing or feeling taken away by your emotions. When this happens, gently acknowledge it without judgment and return to the steps of recognizing sensations, validating emotions, allowing, and soothing.

The beliefs may feel so strongly true they feel like a part of you and color everything. That is okay. Wherever you are right now is just fine. Noticing is a step. This is a process and a journey and an education. You are in the school of you now.

Over time, with consistent practice, you can develop a deeper understanding of your emotional world and respond to challenges with greater resilience and authenticity.

How Do I Know What I Believe?

Authentic Self

Are you considering yourself in the equation?

Authenticity, for our purposes, refers to living in alignment with one's true nature, beliefs, and feelings. It means expressing and honoring who you are at the deepest level, rather than conforming to external expectations or societal norms.

Authenticity is rooted in the core self, the essence of who you are beneath the layers of learned behaviors, roles, and external influences. It involves being in touch with your innermost values, desires, and needs. Living authentically means your actions and decisions come from this core rather than from external pressures or fears.

Authenticity in relation to identity involves acknowledging and embracing all parts of yourself, including those that may not fit neatly into prescribed roles. It's about letting your identity be fluid and evolving, rather than fixed by what others expect or what you think you "should" be. Authenticity allows you to create a sense of identity based on your own understanding and acceptance of who you are.

Being authentic with emotions means allowing yourself to feel and express emotions as they truly are, without suppression or denial. Authentic emotional expression involves recognizing your feelings and being honest about them with yourself and others. It means not hiding or minimizing emotions out of fear of judgment or rejection, but rather allowing them to guide your interactions in a healthy and genuine way.

In essence, authenticity is about living in a way that reflects your true self, emotionally, mentally, and behaviorally, creating a life that feels real and congruent with who you genuinely are.

Authentic core self considers needs of self and personal values before taking action externally.

What Do You Believe, or Values

Are you aligning with your values?

Values help you understand not just what you believe, but who you are beneath survival responses, old narratives, and inherited expectations. They act as a compass for the emotional work you are doing. You cannot choose every emotion that arises, and you cannot control every thought that appears, but you can choose how you want to live, what you stand for, and the qualities you want to embody.

Values represent what matters most to you in a steady and enduring way. Unlike emotions, which shift, or beliefs, which can be shaped by past wounds, values point you toward the person you want to be now. They guide decisions, boundaries, relationships, and how you engage with the world. When beliefs formed in the past conflict with your present-day values, the tension you feel often signals a place where healing is ready to happen.

To begin exploring values, take a moment to reflect on what qualities you admire, what you look for in relationships, and what makes life feel meaningful. Some people value creativity, honesty, compassion, growth, security, curiosity, or kindness. Others may value freedom, belonging, justice, authenticity, or love. There is no right list, only the one that comes from your truest self.

If it feels helpful, you can look at a more complete list of values, such as the one at think2perform.com. Not every value will resonate, but a few will feel like home.

When you have a sense of your values, you can begin to compare them with the beliefs you identified earlier. Ask yourself:

Does this belief align with the person I want to be?

Does it support my well-being, connection, and self-respect?

Would I want a loved one to live by this belief?

Is it rooted in my values, or in a past moment of fear, shame, or powerlessness?

You are not trying to force yourself into positivity. You are simply checking whether the belief you carry belongs with the life you are building now.

Preferred beliefs, which we will explore fully in the next chapter, grow naturally from your values. When you know what is important to you, it becomes easier to recognize which beliefs are remnants of the past and which are aligned with the self you are becoming.

Tending To The Past

The following work can be highly activating to the nervous system. It is best to establish a firm sense of safety in self before looking into the past. It is never wrong to ask for help. If you find the following increases distress, consider using the container exercise to set aside, for the moment, any upsetting thoughts, emotions, and felt sensations.

We are no longer stuffing down our emotional experience but we are allowed to put the work aside as often as we need to. It is enough to notice the belief and move with self-compassion.

During an emotional flashback, the past becomes present. The world is seen through the lens of the belief formed in the past, it feels true now. Engrained responses, that were protective and useful in the past, feel true and needed now.

When we notice the past becoming present, we can send validation, compassion, and all the things we needed and did not get to our past selves. Label the emotions and physical sensations as a remnant from your past and notice that you were not able to feel all you needed to then. Allow that past part of self to feel the feelings trapped in the body.

This experience feels similar to situations in the past where I was unable to express my emotions and my emotional needs were not met. I can sit with the part of myself that had this experience. I can show compassion and empathy. I can soothe and provide kindness and comfort to the past self that did not receive those things. Then I can look on the present without the shade of the past.

Similarly, if we notice and identify the negative belief, we can eventually pinpoint when and how this belief was formed in the past. These were times when we were unable or it was unsafe to express the emotions we were experiencing.

I recognize that what I'm feeling now is connected to a past experience. My body and mind are responding as if the past is happening all over again, but I know I'm here in the present. The beliefs and emotions that come up are remnants of what I needed to protect myself then, and they served me well.

Now, I can see that I wasn't able to fully feel those emotions back then. I can offer my past self the kindness, compassion, and validation that I didn't receive at the time. I can sit with this part of me, allowing it to express the sadness, fear, or anger that couldn't be felt before.

I honor the courage it took to survive that moment. Now, I offer the comfort and safety that I didn't have then, letting this part of me know it's okay to release the pain. As I do this, I allow myself to view the present moment clearly, without the shadows of the past.

Steps During Emotional Flashbacks

Awareness of Shift Away from Baseline

Start learning the cues your body gives when an emotional flashback is occurring. This may be a familiar sensation like tension in your stomach or chest. Notice how your breathing, posture, or energy shifts. Negative intrusive thoughts are another good indicator. These signals are your body's way of letting you know that the past is surfacing.

Label the Emotion

Identify and name the emotion you're feeling: sadness, anger, disgust, fear, or surprise. Recognizing the emotion can help you create space between the feeling and your sense of self.

Acknowledge and Validate the Emotion

Say to yourself: *I am feeling [emotion]. It's okay to feel this way.* Acknowledge the root of the emotion. For example: *I feel scared because, in the past, conflict was unsafe.* By labeling and validating, you're showing understanding and kindness to the part of yourself that was once unable to express these feelings.

Tend to the Emotion Compassionately

Imagine how you would support a friend, a child, or even your past self experiencing this emotion. What words would you offer them? What actions would you take? Now, offer that same compassion to yourself. *It makes sense that I feel this way. I'm here now to comfort and soothe myself. I can give myself what I didn't get before.*

Reorient to Present and Label Experience

Remind yourself, *I am triggered, and the thoughts I'm having about myself aren't true. These beliefs were formed in the past when I needed to protect myself. Right now, I am safe, and I am good enough exactly as I am. My worth is not tied to this moment.*

Implement Soothing Techniques for the Emotion

This includes all the activities mentioned previously for each emotion including grounding, orienting to present, sensory techniques, breathing exercises, co-regulation, rhythmic movement, and so on.

Compassionate Reflection

After you return to your window of tolerance, take a moment to reflect compassionately.

What I just felt was an echo of my past. I can see now that I was reacting from an old place of fear or pain. I honor that part of myself and am grateful for how it helped me survive. Now, I can offer the kindness and safety I needed back then.

This helps to close the experience with validation and soothing, reinforcing your connection to the present.

Orienting Response Exercise: Seeing the World with Adult Glasses

Close your eyes and take a few deep breaths, settling into the present moment. Now, imagine yourself as a child, standing in a place or situation where you once felt overwhelmed. Notice the way your child self views the world, perhaps things seem larger, more daunting, or harder to understand.

Now, in your mind's eye, approach your younger self. You're holding a pair of glasses, your adult glasses. Offer them to your child self and guide them to put them on, allowing them to see through your adult eyes. These glasses are not magical, but they offer adult clarity and perspective to the child.

As your child self gazes through these adult lenses, watch how the world around them shifts. They begin to see with greater understanding, with a new perspective on that which was once frightening or overwhelming. They can see that not all their assessments of threat were accurate, that they no longer have to feel powerless, that they have more choice in how to respond.

Let your child self notice the safety, support, and truth they can find in your adult self. There is security in the present. As they continue to look through these glasses, a sense of calm and clarity washes over them, and they begin to understand the world from your adult perspective, grounded in reality, with the ability to handle what comes.

When you're ready, take a deep breath and bring your awareness back to the present, knowing that you can always reach out to the child to offer adult perspective and comfort.

End Of Chapter Practice: Mapping One Emotional Moment

For this practice, you're not trying to fix anything. You are simply tracing one small moment from body, to emotion, to thought, to belief. Think of it as making a sketch, not a finished portrait.

Choose one recent moment that still has emotional charge. It does not have to be a crisis. It could be a comment someone made, a text that stung, a silence that felt heavy, a small success uncelebrated.

Take a few breaths and bring the moment to mind. Let yourself remember where you were, who else was there, what was happening around you. Then, shift your attention to your body. Notice what happens inside as you recall it. Do you feel tightness, heaviness, heat, numbness, buzzing, a drop, a lift? Let the body speak first.

See if you can name the core emotion that fits the sensations most closely: anger, sadness, fear, disgust, surprise, or enjoyment. There is no prize for getting it "right." You are just practicing language for what your body already knows.

Now, listen for the first thought that comes with this emotion. It might sound like a sentence. It might be a quick image or a familiar phrase. *I always mess this up. No one ever listens. This is my fault. This will not last.* Write that thought down or say it quietly to yourself.

From there, gently wonder what belief might sit underneath this thought. If this thought were part of a deeper story about you or the world, what might it be. *I am not good enough. I am not safe. I have no choices. I do not matter. I am alone.* Let it take the form of an "I am" or "The world is" sentence if that feels natural. If nothing clear comes, that is okay. The wondering itself is part of the practice.

Once you have a possible belief, pause and notice how your body responds to it. Does something tighten, sink, brace, or pull away? Does anything soften because it finally has words? You are not arguing with the belief here, only noticing how deeply it might live in you.

If the belief feels supportive, you can bring in your values. Ask yourself: *Does this belief match the way I would like to see myself, others, or the world? Would I want someone I love to hold this belief about themselves?* You are not forcing a new belief, you are simply holding the old one up next to what is important to you.

If at any point the exploration feels too intense, imagine placing the moment, the thought, and the belief into your container, to be returned to later when you have more support. You are allowed to stop after any step. Even noticing one hard thought and the emotion that came with it is enough.

Close the practice by placing a hand over your heart or another place that feels steady. Offer yourself one sentence that feels true enough for right now. Something like: *It makes sense that I feel this way. I am learning more about what I carry. I am allowed to go slowly.*

You can repeat this practice with different moments over time. Each small map you make will help you see how your body, emotions, thoughts, and beliefs move together, and it will prepare the ground for the preferred beliefs you will explore in the next chapter.

Moving Toward Preferred Beliefs

Objective: Identify and move toward preferred beliefs.

A belief is only a thought you continue to think. A belief is nothing more than a chronic pattern of thought, and you have the ability—if you try even a little bit—to begin a new pattern, to tell a new story, to achieve a different vibration, to change your point of attraction. – Abraham Hicks

Regulation In The Context Of Emotions

Regulation (in the context of this work) is a harmonious connection, with awareness and flow, between the physical body, thoughts, and emotional states. It entails an ability to notice and interpret bodily cues alongside their associated thoughts. Regulation further involves fostering tolerance and understanding of these internal signals, facilitating a balanced and adaptive response to experience.

Experiencing Something Different

Change begins when the body has an experience that does not match what it has come to expect. Over time, repeated emotional experiences shape patterns of response, creating a sense of what feels familiar or likely to happen next. When something different occurs, and we are able to notice and stay with it, even briefly, it can begin to loosen these patterns. In this way, new experiences in the body can create space for more flexibility, allowing for different responses to emerge.

Visualization

Visualization is imagining, sensing, or reflecting on a situation as if it were happening right now. The goal isn't to force imagery but to allow your nervous system to gently explore what it might feel like to experience something different than what you learned in childhood. Visualization helps the body and mind rehearse new responses before taking action, creating a bridge between insight and change. It becomes a safe way to begin softening the grip of old beliefs and making space for something new.

Example 1: Trust

Imagine you grew up believing people were untrustworthy. Bring to mind someone who has felt unpredictable or unsafe and notice what happens in your body as you do. You might feel tension, tightening, or a sense of pulling back. Then, shift your attention to someone who has felt more steady or reliable and notice what changes, even slightly. There may be a softening, a small exhale, or a subtle sense of ease. Gently move your awareness back and forth between these two experiences, simply noticing the differences without needing to change anything. If it feels possible, allow both experiences to be present at the same time and notice what happens in your body as they coexist.

Example 2: Not good enough

Imagine you grew up with the sense that you are not good enough. Bring to mind a moment where that feeling was strong and notice how it shows up in your body. You might feel heaviness, constriction, or a pulling inward. Then, bring to mind a moment where you felt capable, appreciated, or seen, even in a small way, and notice what shifts in your body. There may be a lightness, warmth, or a slight sense of expansion. Gently move between these two experiences, noticing the difference in sensation without needing to resolve it. If it feels possible, allow both to be present at once and notice what happens in your body as these experiences sit side by side.

Example 3: Safety

Imagine you grew up in an environment that felt unpredictable or unsafe. Bring to mind a moment or place where your body felt on edge and notice the sensations that arise. There may be tension, alertness, or a sense of bracing. Then, bring to mind a place or moment where your body felt even slightly more at ease and notice any softening, slowing, or settling. Gently move your attention between these two experiences, noticing how your body responds to each. If it feels possible, allow both to be present in your awareness at the same time and notice what happens in your body as both experiences exist together.

Moving Toward Preferred Beliefs For Each Emotion

The following practices are about offering your nervous system a new possibility and rehearsing it in small, lived ways. Old beliefs became wired in you through repeated emotional experiences. New beliefs need the same repetition, paired with regulation and compassion.

For each core emotion, you will move through three layers: notice the old belief, name a preferred belief, and try one tiny action to move in that direction. You do not have to be completely convinced by the new belief to make change. The act of turning toward it and taking a small step is the work.

Fear

When fear shows up as a racing heart, shallow breath, or a sense that something terrible is about to happen, the belief beneath it often sounds like, *I am not safe,* or *I cannot handle this,* or *the world is dangerous and unpredictable.*

A preferred belief might sound like, *some things are hard and I can meet them,* or *I can create pockets of safety for myself, even when I feel afraid.*

After grounding your body, you can gently ask what a person with this belief might do next. They might look around the room and name three things that signal safety. They might take one step toward a task while feeling scared. They might ask for support instead of facing everything alone.

Choose one tiny action that says, *I am here with myself in this fear.* You are not demanding that fear vanish. You are teaching your nervous system that it does not have to face everything alone.

Sadness

When sadness brings heaviness, a lump in the throat, or the urge to disappear, the belief underneath often sounds like, *my feelings are too much,* or *no one will stay if I show this,* or *my needs are a burden.*

A preferred belief might be, *my sadness is allowed,* or *I am worthy of care even when I am struggling.*

After soothing your body in whatever way is available, imagine how someone who believed this might tend to themselves. Perhaps they let a tear fall instead of swallowing it. Perhaps they text a trusted person instead of isolating. Maybe they put a blanket over their shoulders or make tea as a sign that their pain is allowed.

Choose one small act of kindness toward your sadness and let it stand as evidence that your feelings are not too much for you. The belief will not shift all at once, but your body will begin to learn that sadness can exist alongside care.

Anger

When anger rises and you notice heat, pressure, or the urge to explode or shut down, you can pause and wonder what story about you has awakened. Often the underlying belief sounds like, *It is not safe to express my needs* or *I am not heard unless I push,* or *my needs do not matter unless I fight for them.*

A preferred belief might sound like, *my needs matter and deserve to be heard,* or *I can express my anger without harming myself or others.*

After your body is more regulated, imagine one small way a person who holds that belief might respond. Maybe they take one breath before speaking. Maybe they say, *I need a moment,* instead of slamming a door. Maybe they state one clear request in a calm tone. Choose just one of these and try it in a low-stakes moment. Let your body feel what it is like to be angry and still stay connected to yourself.

You are not erasing anger. You are offering it a new path to travel.

Disgust

When disgust curls you away from something, tightens your stomach, or fills you with a sharp urge to reject, the belief that rises often sounds like, *I have no control here,* or *if I get too close, I will be contaminated or harmed,* or *parts of me or others are unacceptable.*

A preferred belief might sound like, *my disgust is trying to protect me and I can choose how to respond,* or *I can honor my boundaries without turning against myself.*

After the intensity has softened, imagine how someone who holds that belief might move. They might take one step back from a situation that feels too close, then check in with their values. They might say, *this is not for me,* without shaming themselves or others. They might offer a gentle reminder to self: *I can choose what I take in.*

Pick one small response that respects your disgust as a signal but does not let it decide everything. Over time, your body can learn that you have more choice than the old belief allowed.

Surprise

When surprise jolts your system, startles your body, or sends a quick burst of energy through you, the old belief often sounds like, *I must always be prepared, if I am caught off guard, I will be hurt or shamed,* or *I am only safe if I control everything.*

A preferred belief might sound like, *unexpected things can happen and I can adjust,* or *I can pause and check what is actually happening before I decide what it means.*

After your body settles from the initial startle, imagine one way someone with this belief might respond. They might take one slow breath before reacting. They might ask a clarifying question instead of assuming the worst. They might say to themselves, *I did not see that coming and I can still choose my next step.*

Choose one small pause or question you can bring into surprising moments. Each time you do, you are loosening the old rule that you must control everything to be safe.

Enjoyment

When enjoyment brings warmth, lightness, or bright energy, the attached belief often sounds like, *I do not deserve this, if I relax, something bad will happen,* or *it is selfish to feel good when others are struggling.*

A preferred belief might sound like, *joy is allowed, even in small moments,* or *my enjoyment can coexist with care for others.*

After noticing and savoring the physical sensation of enjoyment, you might imagine how someone who holds this belief would stay with it. Maybe they let themselves take one more sip, one more breath, one more minute of sunlight. Maybe they share the good moment with someone else instead of hiding it. Maybe they say quietly inside, *this is for me too.*

Choose one small way to stay with or share the joy instead of shrinking away from it. You are not forcing yourself to be happy. You are letting your nervous system discover that enjoyment is not a trap, but a resource.

Moving Toward Preferred Beliefs General

Let's say you're dealing with a recurring pattern of feeling inadequate in your work. You've been practicing the techniques outlined here, like breathwork, body scans, and identifying the core emotions that arise. However, you notice that whenever you receive constructive criticism, even if it's delivered gently and with good intentions, you feel a wave of shame wash over you. Your heart starts to race, your palms get sweaty, and you feel a pit in your stomach. You successfully identify this as fear, fear of not being good enough, fear of judgment, and fear of failure.

By allowing yourself to sit with this fear, without trying to push it away or immediately fix it, you start to notice the thoughts swirling in your mind. These thoughts might sound something like:

I'm not cut out for this job.

Everyone else is more competent than me.

I'm going to be found out as a fraud.

I am not good enough.

You recognize these thoughts as echoes of deeply held negative core beliefs, potentially rooted in childhood experiences or past situations where you felt inadequate. Perhaps you had a caregiver who was highly critical, or you experienced a significant setback that left you feeling insecure about your abilities.

By creating space for your fear and acknowledging the accompanying thoughts without judgment, you've already begun the process of shifting these beliefs. You've brought them from the shadows of your subconscious into the light of awareness. This awareness is crucial because it allows you to start questioning these beliefs.

Is it really true that I'm not good enough? Is there evidence to support this belief?

What if I chose to view this criticism as an opportunity for growth, rather than confirmation of my inadequacy?

As you continue to practice the techniques, you might decide to challenge these negative beliefs more directly. You could use affirmations to cultivate a more empowering perspective, repeating phrases like.

I am capable and constantly learning.

I am open to feedback and growth.

By acknowledging your emotions, identifying the underlying beliefs, and intentionally choosing more supportive perspectives, you've set the stage for lasting transformation. Over time, with consistent practice, you may find that the intensity of your fear lessens, and you're able to approach challenges with greater self-compassion and resilience.

Activity: Envisioning Successful Action

This exercise focuses on creating a felt sense of confidence and ease through visualization and body awareness. The goal is to connect with your body's natural capacity for safety and capability, reinforcing the experience on a somatic level before taking action.

Set the Scene

Find a comfortable position where you can remain alert yet relaxed. Let your breath settle into a steady rhythm. Before imagining any scenario, take a moment to notice how your body feels right now. Do you feel tension anywhere? Ease? Neutrality? Simply observe.

Imagine the Sensation of Readiness

Before visualizing a specific action, recall a time, any time, you felt capable, calm, or even just neutral in your body. It could be as simple as walking outside, finishing a task, or a moment of stillness. Where do you feel that sensation in your body? If it had a texture, weight, or movement, what would it be like?

Visualize the Experience

Now, picture yourself in a situation where you'd like to respond differently, perhaps setting a boundary, speaking confidently, or engaging in something new. Instead of focusing on what you say or do first, imagine how you *feel* in that moment. How does your body hold itself? What physical sensations accompany a sense of steadiness? Maybe it's a solid stance, a gentle breath, or warmth in your chest.

Enhance the Positive Physical Sensations

As you continue to visualize yourself in the scenario, subtly adjust your posture or breath in real life to match the sensation of confidence or ease. Maybe you sit a little taller, soften your shoulders, or deepen your exhale. If a color, texture, or image emerges, let it be a resource, something you can return to when needed.

Ground into the Experience

Before opening your eyes, take a moment to *store* this felt sense. You might gently press your fingertips together, place a hand on your chest, or take one deep breath to reinforce the connection between your body and the experience of capability.

Repeat and Integrate

This exercise is most powerful when practiced regularly, allowing your body to become more familiar with the sensation of readiness. The more you engage with this felt sense, the easier it becomes to access in real-world situations.

Putting Preferred Beliefs Into Action

This exercise bridges the gap between insight and action, helping you take tangible steps that align with your preferred beliefs.

Identify a Challenging Belief

What belief tends to arise in moments of distress? It might be about yourself, your relationships, or the world. Choose one that feels relevant but workable.

Craft a Preferred Belief

Frame a new belief that feels possible, even if not fully integrated yet. Instead of *I am completely confident,* you might say, *I am learning to trust myself.* The belief should feel like a small shift, not an unreachable ideal.

Choose a Real-World Action

Instead of focusing on *how you think*, focus on *how you act*. What is one small action that embodies this preferred belief? Keep it simple and achievable, such as offering yourself kind words when self-doubt arises. Holding eye contact when speaking. Taking a break without guilt. Expressing an opinion, even in a low-stakes situation.

Take the Action with Awareness

As you move through the action, notice any shifts in sensation. Does your breath quicken? Do you feel tension or ease? Observe with curiosity rather than judgment. If discomfort arises, remind yourself that change feels unfamiliar, not wrong.

Reflect and Reinforce

Afterward, pause and acknowledge what happened, not whether it was "perfect," but that you did something different. What felt different? What did your body experience? Each small shift builds momentum, reinforcing new patterns over time.

Examples for Specific Beliefs

I am not good enough.

Set the scene: Take a few deep breaths to center yourself. Think about a belief you would like to hold about yourself, something that feels empowering, even if it feels unrealistic right now. It could be, *I am good enough exactly as I am.*

Imagine: Close your eyes and imagine what it would be like to truly hold this belief. Picture someone who believes this about themselves. How would they act, respond, and carry themselves in the world? What would they say in challenging situations?

Pick a response: Choose just one small way they might respond differently. Maybe they speak up confidently, smile at themselves in the mirror, or set a small boundary.

Affirmation: Ask yourself, *what if I truly believed this? How would it feel in my body?* Allow yourself to feel into this belief, bringing up any sensations of ease, warmth, or comfort. If it feels difficult, that's okay, just notice the resistance without judgment.

Take a baby step: Now, pick a tiny step you could take toward that response. Maybe it's writing down an affirmation or practicing that smile in the mirror. Even the smallest movement is significant.

Reflect: After you've taken your baby step, reflect on how it felt.

You can repeat this process regularly to build momentum, knowing that small steps can eventually lead to bigger shifts.

I cannot trust myself.

Set the scene: Take a few deep breaths to center yourself. Think about a belief you would like to hold about yourself related to self-trust, something that feels empowering, even if it feels unrealistic right now. It could be, *I trust my intuition and judgment.*

Imagine: Close your eyes and imagine what it would be like to genuinely hold this belief. Picture someone who trusts themselves deeply. How would they act, respond, and carry themselves in the world? What would they say in challenging situations that require a decision?

Pick a response: Choose just one small way they might respond differently. Maybe they pause before making a decision, tuning into their gut feeling, rather than immediately seeking external validation. Or perhaps they set a boundary with someone, honoring their inner voice, even if it feels a bit uncomfortable.

Affirmation: Ask yourself, *what if I truly believed this? What sensations arise when I connect with a feeling of trust in my body?* Allow yourself to feel into this belief, bringing up any sensations of groundedness, stability, or a sense of inner knowing. If it feels difficult, that's okay — just notice the resistance without judgment.

Take a baby step: Now, pick a tiny step you could take toward that response. Maybe it's taking a moment of quiet reflection before making a decision that feels significant or practicing saying *no* to a small request that doesn't align with your needs. Even the smallest movement is significant.

Reflect: After you've taken your baby step, reflect on how it felt to access a new response. Did you notice any internal shifts as you practiced trusting your intuition? Were there any thoughts or sensations that came up? You can repeat this process regularly to build momentum, knowing that small steps can eventually lead to bigger shifts.

I am responsible for other people's emotions.

Set the scene: Take a few slow breaths and allow your body to settle. Bring to mind a belief you would like to hold about yourself related to emotional responsibility. It might be something like, *I can care about others without being responsible for how they feel*, or *I am allowed to have my own experience even when others are upset.*

Imagine: Close your eyes and imagine what it would be like to hold this belief. Picture someone who can stay present with others without taking on their emotions. How do they respond when someone around them is upset, disappointed, or overwhelmed? Notice their posture, their tone, the way they stay connected without overextending themselves.

Pick a response: Choose one small way they might respond differently. Maybe they pause instead of rushing to fix or smooth things over. Perhaps they listen without immediately taking responsibility, or they allow a moment of silence instead of filling the space. It might be as simple as noticing the urge to fix and not acting on it right away.

Affirmation: Ask yourself, *what if I did not have to carry this? What if I could stay present without taking it on?* Notice what sensations arise in your body as you consider this. There may be a sense of space, a softening, or even discomfort. Allow whatever is there to be present without needing to change it.

Take a baby step: Choose a small, manageable step that moves in this direction. This might be allowing someone to have their reaction without intervening, or pausing before responding when you feel the urge to take responsibility. Keep it small enough that it feels possible.

Reflect: Afterward, take a moment to notice what it was like to respond differently. What did you feel in your body? Did anything shift, even slightly? Were there moments of ease, tension, or uncertainty? Simply notice. Over time, these small experiences can begin to create more space between you and the belief that you are responsible for others' emotions.

I am not worthy of love and connection unless I am perfect.

Set the scene: Take a few deep breaths to center yourself. Think about a belief you would like to hold about yourself around vulnerability, something that feels empowering, even if it feels unrealistic right now. It could be, *I am worthy of love and connection, even when I am imperfect.*

Imagine: Close your eyes and imagine what it would be like to truly hold this belief. Picture someone who embraces their vulnerability. How would they act, respond, and carry themselves in relationships? What would they do differently?

Pick a Response: Choose just one small way they might respond differently. Maybe they share a personal story with a trusted friend, revealing a part of themselves they usually keep hidden. Or perhaps they allow themselves to receive a compliment without deflecting or downplaying it.

Affirmation: Ask yourself, *what if I truly believed I was worthy of love, even in my imperfection? What would that feel like in my body?* Allow yourself to feel into this belief, bringing up any sensations of warmth, openness, or a sense of belonging. If it feels difficult, that's okay, just notice the resistance without judgment.

Take a baby step: Now, pick a tiny step you could take toward that response. Maybe it's expressing appreciation to a loved one or allowing yourself to receive a kind gesture without feeling the need to reciprocate immediately. Even the smallest movement is important.

Reflect: After you've taken your baby step, reflect on how it felt. Did you notice any shifts in your body or thoughts? You can repeat this process regularly to build momentum, knowing that small steps can eventually lead to bigger shifts.

I am unsafe.

Set the scene: Take a few deep breaths to center yourself. Think about a belief you would like to hold about yourself related to safety, something that feels empowering, even if it feels unrealistic right now. This belief could be, *I am safe and I can trust my instincts.*

Imagine: Close your eyes and imagine what it would be like to genuinely hold this belief. Picture someone who feels safe and grounded. How would they act, respond, and carry themselves in the world? How would they respond to potential threats or situations that make them feel uneasy?

Pick a Response: Choose just one small way they might respond differently. Perhaps, rather than immediately going into fight or flight mode, they pause, take a deep breath, and tune into their body's signals. Maybe they notice their surroundings, checking in with their senses to assess if there's a real threat, or if their body is reacting based on past experiences.

Affirmation: Ask yourself, *what if I truly believed I was safe? What sensations would tell me that I am safe?* Allow yourself to feel into this belief, bringing up any sensations of relaxation, ease, or a sense of being held and supported. If it feels difficult, that's okay, just notice the resistance without judgment. You might even imagine a blue dot, using it as a visual anchor to bring your attention back to a sense of calm.

Take a baby step: Now, pick a tiny step you could take toward that response. Maybe it's practicing a grounding exercise next time you feel unsafe or noticing the safe and comforting things around you. It could even be as simple as placing a blue dot somewhere you'll see it regularly, as a visual reminder to connect with your breath and a sense of safety. Even the smallest movement is important.

Reflect: After you've taken your baby step, reflect on how it felt. Did you notice any shifts in your body or thoughts? Did you find it easier to connect with a sense of safety, even if it was just for a moment? You can repeat this process regularly to build momentum, knowing that small steps can eventually lead to bigger shifts.

Remember, the goal is not to force yourself to feel safe when you genuinely don't, especially in situations of actual danger. Instead, these exercises are designed to help you cultivate a greater sense of safety within yourself over time, by bringing awareness to your body's signals and gently shifting your responses to align with your preferred belief.

Shifting ingrained beliefs is a process, not a destination. Some days will feel easier than others, and that's okay. The most important thing is to approach this journey with kindness and patience for yourself, honoring each step you take toward greater alignment with your preferred beliefs.

End Of Chapter Practice: One Small Step Toward A Preferred Belief

Choose one belief that you have noticed. It might be about you, about others, or about the world. Pick something familiar but workable, not the heaviest belief you hold.

Find a comfortable position and let your breath settle. Take a moment to notice how your body feels right now without trying to change it. Then bring to mind a recent situation where this belief showed up. Notice what emotion was present and where you felt it in your body. Let the memory be clear enough to feel, but not so vivid that you become overwhelmed. If it feels too intense, move to a milder example.

Silently name the belief that rises with this situation. It might sound like, *I am not good enough,* or *I cannot trust myself,* or *I am unsafe,* or *I am unlovable.* You do not have to argue with it yet. Simply acknowledge, *this is the story that comes up here.*

Now, imagine a preferred belief that you would like to move toward, even if it does not feel fully true. Soften the wording until it feels possible. Instead of *I am completely confident,* you might say, *I am learning to trust myself.* Instead of *I am always safe,* you might say, *right now I can check what is actually happening.*

Take a breath and ask yourself, *if I believed this just a little more, how would my body hold itself? Would my shoulders shift? Would my breath feel different? Would my gaze soften or steady?* Make a small adjustment in your posture to match this imagined belief. Let your body try it on.

From here, imagine one tiny action that fits with the preferred belief. It might be speaking one sentence, asking one question, pausing for one breath, sending one text, or offering yourself one kind phrase. Choose an action small enough that it feels doable, even if you feel unsure.

Make a quiet commitment to try this action the next time a similar situation arises. You are not promising perfection. You are simply agreeing to experiment. If you like, anchor this intention in your body by placing a hand on your chest or pressing your fingertips together while you think of the action.

When you are finished, take a moment to thank yourself for your willingness to see your belief clearly. You do not have to feel different right now for this to be important. You are showing your nervous system another path, one small step at a time.

You can return to this practice with the same belief many times, or choose a new one as you feel ready. Repetition is how old learning was written in you. Repetition, with compassion, is also how you can write a new story.

Loving-Kindness Meditation (Metta)

This practice involves cultivating feelings of love and compassion, first for oneself and then extending outward to others. This practice can help counter self-criticism, promote self-acceptance, and increase feelings of connection and kindness.

Begin by finding a comfortable position.

Sit or lie down, allowing your body to relax and settle into the present moment. Close your eyes if it feels comfortable, and take a few deep breaths.

Feel your body resting on the surface beneath you, and notice the sensation of the air as you inhale and exhale.

Start by bringing your attention inward.

Place your hand gently on your heart if that feels soothing. Begin to silently repeat the following phrases, focusing on your well-being:

May I be happy.

May I be healthy.

May I be safe.

May I live with ease.

As you say each phrase, take a moment to pause and allow yourself to feel the meaning of the words. Imagine warmth and love filling your heart as you offer yourself kindness and care.

Now, think of someone you love.

Bring to mind someone who is easy for you to care about. This could be a close friend, family member, or even a pet. Visualize this person in your mind, and silently repeat the same loving-kindness phrases for them:

May you be happy.

May you be healthy.

May you be safe.

May you live with ease.

Feel your heart open as you send warmth and love to this person. Visualize them receiving your well wishes and being surrounded by peace.

Next, bring to mind someone neutral.

This could be someone you see regularly but don't know well, such as a colleague, neighbor, or the cashier at your local store. Picture them in your mind, and extend the same loving-kindness phrases to them:

May you be happy.

May you be healthy.

May you be safe.

May you live with ease.

Notice how it feels to offer kindness to someone with whom you don't have a strong emotional connection. Allow yourself to wish them well, just as you would for a close loved one.

Now, think of someone with whom you've had difficulty.

This may feel challenging, and that's okay. Choose someone with whom you've experienced conflict or discomfort, but who is not too emotionally charged for you at this moment. Picture them in your mind and repeat the same phrases, offering them kindness:

May you be happy.

May you be healthy.

May you be safe.

May you live with ease.

If feelings of resistance or discomfort arise, notice them without judgment. Remember that offering loving-kindness to others doesn't mean condoning harmful behavior; it's about cultivating compassion for all beings, including those who challenge us.

Finally, extend loving-kindness to all beings.

Imagine sending waves of warmth and love out into the world, touching every living being. Silently repeat:

May all beings be happy.

May all beings be healthy.

May all beings be safe.

May all beings live with ease.

Visualize the entire world filled with peace, joy, and compassion.

Take a few more deep breaths.

Let this feeling of loving-kindness settle in your body. When you're ready, slowly open your eyes, and carry this sense of compassion and warmth with you throughout your day.

"The Most Important Thing"

by Julia Fehrenbacher, used with her kind permission.
Originally published on juliafehrenbacher.com

I am making a home inside myself.

A shelter

of kindness where everything

is forgiven, everything allowed — a quiet patch

of sunlight to stretch out without hurry,

where all that has been banished

and buried is welcomed, spoken, listened to — released.

A fiercely friendly place I can claim as my very own.

I am throwing arms open

to the whole of myself—especially the fearful,
fault-finding, falling apart, unfinished parts, knowing
every seed and weed, every drop
of rain, has made the soil richer.

I will light a candle, pour a hot cup of tea, gather
around the warmth of my own blazing fire. I will howl
if I want to, knowing this flame can burn through
any perceived problem, any prescribed perfectionism,
any lying limitation, every heavy thing.

I am making a home inside myself
where grace blooms in grand and glorious
abundance, a shelter of kindness that grows
all the truest things.

I whisper hallelujah to the friendly
sky. Watch now as I burst into blossom.
—Julia Fehrenbacher

Acknowledgments

"You like me, you really like me?" – Sally Field

This book would not exist without the people who have allowed me to witness their inner worlds, the loved ones who have supported me along the way, my own challenges and struggles, and you, the reader.

It feels difficult to fully express my gratitude here. There is something about trying to put appreciation into words that never quite captures it. Still, thank you for being here, for choosing this book, and for staying with it and me.

To my clients, thank you for trusting me with your stories and your inner worlds. The ways you have stayed with yourself, even in moments that felt overwhelming, have deeply shaped how I understand this work. It is an honor to witness your courage, your honesty, and your willingness to experience something different.

To the teachers, writers, and clinicians who have shaped my understanding of the body, emotions, and healing, thank you. Your work lives within these pages in ways both direct and subtle, and I hope I have honored each of you here.

To my colleagues and community, thank you for the conversations, the shared language, and the commitment to creating spaces where people can feel safe enough to be fully human.

To my children, thank you for your forgiveness, your love, and for allowing me to grow and do better. You have taught me more than I could have learned any other way. To my friends, thank you for listening, encouraging, and walking alongside me. To my husband, thank you for believing in me and in my ability to write this, and for being my first reader. I love each of you so much.

To my mom, thank you for the ways you allowed me to walk alongside you in finding moments of peace within anxiety. That experience shaped not only this work, but also how I have come to understand my own. I love you and miss you.

I am especially grateful to Julia Fehrenbacher for granting permission to include her poem “The Most Important Thing” in this book.

And to you, dear reader, thank you for sitting here a spell, with me, your emotions, and yourself. So much love to you. I believe in you! You've got this.

www.ingramcontent.com/pod-product-compliance
Lightning Source LLC
LaVergne TN
LVHW081259100826
845148LV00005B/917

* 9 7 9 8 2 3 4 0 5 0 3 8 0 *